FACING APOCALYPSE

DAVID MILLER
ROBERT JAY LIFTON
DENISE LEVERTOV
MARY WATKINS
WOLFGANG GIEGERICH
DANILO DOLCI
JAMES HILLMAN
NORMAN O. BROWN
JOANNA MACY
MIKE PERLMAN

FACING APOCALYPSE

edited by
VALERIE ANDREWS
ROBERT BOSNAK
KAREN WALTER GOODWIN

Spring Publications, Inc.
Dallas, Texas

Published by Spring Publications, Inc.; P.O. Box 222069; Dallas, Texas 75222. Printed in the United States of America

The cover image is a detail from the photograph "Public Domain" (1982), originally a Polaroid Land print, 20" x 24", which was taken by Rosamond W. Purcell and appears by courtesy of the artist, who exhibits at the Marcuse Pfeifer Gallery in New York City. Patricia Mora and Maribeth Lipscomb designed and produced the cover, and Mary Vernon provided color guidance.

International distributors:
Spring; Postfach; 8800 Thalwil; Switzerland.
Japan Spring Sha, Inc.; 1–2–4, Nishisakaidani-Cho; Ohharano, Nishikyo-Ku; Kyoto, 610–11, Japan.
Element Books Ltd; Longmead Shaftesbury; Dorset SP7 8PL; England.

Library of Congress Cataloging-in-Publication Data

Facing apocalypse.

Includes bibliographies.
1. End of the world—Miscellanea. I. Miller, David LeRoy. II. Andrews, Valerie. III. Bosnak, Robert. IV. Goodwin, Karen Walter.
BF1999.F22 1987 001.9 86–31602
ISBN 0–88214–329–8

To Salve Regina

CONTENTS

Acknowledgments

Salve Regina College made the Facing Apocalypse conference possible. Imagination in Action, a non-profit organization, helped organize, finance and make manifest the vision of Robert Bosnak to create a conference that would bring together professionals of the imagination and public policy makers to address the question: How does psychological awareness alter the pressure of the apocalyptic imagination on our actions?

We have many people to thank, whose hard work, sacrifices, spirit and dedication not only made the conference a success, but also made the preparation of this book possible.

Officers of Imagination in Action:

Carl Barchi, M.Ed.
Financial Planner
Scituate, Rhode Island

Robert Bosnak, J.D.
Jungian Psychoanalyst
Sudbury, Massachusetts

Karen Walter Goodwin
President
Fifth Avenue Productions
New York, New York

Henry E. Kates
President
Mutual Benefit Life Insurance Co.
New York, New York

In addition to the officers, the conference planning committee included:

Thomas Flanagan
Director of Administration
Salve Regina–The Newport College

James Hersh, Ph.D.
Professor of Philosophy
Salve Regina–The Newport College

Deanne Lemle
Movement Therapist
Sudbury, Massachusetts

Sister Sheila Megley, Ph.D.
Vice-President, Academic Dean
Salve Regina–The Newport College

Sherman Teichman, M.A.
Adjunct Professor Mass Communications
and Social Sciences
Emerson College, Boston

We would also like to thank Sister Esther and Sister Lucille McKillop, President of Salve Regina.

The sponsors of the conference include: Salve Regina College; Robert Bosnak; H. Carr and Sons, Providence, Rhode Island; Karen Goodwin; Piccerelli & Gilstein & Co., Providence; Joseph A. Chazan, M.D., Providence; Henry Kates; and Deanne Lemle.

Interpreters:

Anthony Oldcorn, Ph.D.
Professor of Italian Studies
Brown University

Claude L. Campellone, M.A.
President, Promot, Inc.
Providence, Rhode Island

Excluding the question and answer sessions, all the presentations made at the conference appear in this volume and in the order they were delivered. The editors also gratefully acknowledge the essays written by Joanna Macy and Mike Perlman, which were not presented at the conference but were rather requested by Robert Bosnak to aid the reader in better understanding the issues.

We are especially grateful to Mary Helen Sullivan, the managing editor of Spring Publications, who has been a tireless, professional, patient guide through the travails of publishing.

Karen Walter Goodwin
New York City

Introduction
Re-Imagining the End of the World

ROBERT BOSNAK

The nuclear arsenal calls forth ancient images of the end, evoking dreams and nightmares of apocalypse from a variety of cultures. Humankind had dreamt these violent endings long before the technological revolution presented us with nuclear potency, and these images have been returned to us the world over in mythology and folklore. Why face them now?

First, we have seen how political actions grow from collective dreams—dreams that can turn to catastrophic nightmares. In Nazi Germany, for example, the dream of cleansing the Aryan spirit drove people to erase millions of lives in a national mania for "purification."

Second, a careful scrutiny of dreams and images of apocalypse may make us more sensitive to nuclear war—and to those psychological projections which threaten to erupt in an *irreversible* explosion of hostility.

"Facing Apocalypse" was organized to reflect upon those imaginal forces behind the nuclear drive, and to explore those hidden impulses and anxieties connected to the bomb. Held June 1983 in Newport, Rhode Island, at Salve Regina College, the conference assembled poets and social reformers, along with experts in religion, philosophy, and imaginal psychology. The audience of 150 included a radical mix of peace activists, teachers, clergy, and officers from Newport's Naval War College.

Among the chief questions at "Facing Apocalypse" were:

How do we move beyond our Judaeo-Christian vision of the end that is linked to redemption and messianic vengeance? How is this battle between good and evil pitted against our hope for a better world? How can we, as individuals, deal with the tension between the real destruction of the world and our imagination of it?

This book, an outgrowth of the "Facing Apocalypse" conference, presents several brilliant and courageous attempts to illuminate our obsession with world-endings. From a variety of perspectives, it examines our potential to destroy the earth, not only because we have the scientific capability, but simply because this scenario is embedded within the realm of human *imagination*.

Since the early days of psychoanalysis, some hundred years ago, it has been clear to students of depth psychology that our conscious mind is under pressure from forces of the unconscious imagination. Emotional states hover outside our awareness and influence our conscious moods and actions. Dreams, said Freud, are the main access to this region beyond consciousness. In dreams we express our hopes, fears, goals and fascinations, our traumas, loves and hatreds. In dreams we meet what is kept hidden from us in the daylight. In dreams we face our unknown selves.

Psychology has explored this unknown realm of the soul in order to heal the individual. Now in the nuclear age, we may need to create a form of cultural therapy, a way of examining the dreams and visions that impel humanity as a whole toward self-destruction.

If our political actions are blinded by projection, one mistake could cost the world. Yet apocalyptic imagery is so volatile that it even clouds our everyday reactions. An example from analytical practice illustrates this clearly. A man dreams:

> I am living on a very small island, all by myself. It is desert-like. I have a vague feeling that people are far away. Then I see on the horizon the Mushroom Cloud of Fire. I see it coming closer. I know this is the end of the world.

Imagine a person, insulated on a tiny island, a desert world of loneliness. No others around. Such is the world-ending for this man. What happens if this image of burning and bombed-outness remains unhealed and outside the man's conscious awareness? If he refuses or is unable to feel the pain inherent in this image, he may project it onto the world around him, feel that everyone is out to hurt and finally destroy him. This may result in aggressive behavior which he rationalizes as *defensive:* "I am attacked, therefore I must defend myself."

Myths of apocalypse are potent enough to have kept themselves alive for thousands of years. Yet today a new myth of apocalypse is emererging. I once heard a scientist who had been present at the detonation of atomic test bombs compare the explosion of light with the color of a crucified Christ painted by Matthias Grüne-wald. At this juncture, the ancient myth and the nuclear reality unite.

The Indian philosopher Yogananda wrote in 1946, a year after Hiroshima and Nagasaki:

> The human mind can and must liberate within itself energies greater than those within stones and metals, lest the material atomic giant, newly unleashed, turn on the world in mindless destruction.

The theme of "Facing Apocalypse" is this transformation of the individual and collective psyche, along with the need to discover ritual and symbolic endings that will keep us from acting out the literal destruction of the world. Of course, there are no easy answers. Perhaps for now we should do as the poet Rainer Maria Rilke advised and simply "learn to live the questions."

The approaches to re-imagining apocalypse presented in this volume are rich and varied. The urgency of such creative questioning is clear. In the nuclear age, humankind cannot afford to fall once more into a destructive mania caused by mythical projection. We would not recover.

DAVID MILLER

David Miller, Ph.D., is Watson-Ledden Professor of Religion at Syracuse University. Born in 1936 in Ohio, Dr. Miller is internationally known for his studies of the modern religious imagination, on which he has lectured since 1975 at the Eranos Conferences in Ascona, Switzerland. His publications include *Christs: Meditations on Archetypal Images in Theology* and *Gods and Games: Toward a Theology of Play.* In *The New Polytheism,* he calls for a wider vision of humanity and its Gods than is provided by narrow, monotheistic thinking. His most recent work is *Three Faces of God: Traces of the Trinity in Literature and Life.*

Chiliasm
Apocalyptic with a Thousand Faces

"Facing Apocalypse!" Already the matter is difficult before we begin, for there is a double-sally in our theme's title, and it makes a single, secure sense of meaning impossible.

Facing means "facing up to something," something like the so-called "facts of life," not to mention death and dying, looking it in the "face," having courage, calling a spade a deadly spade, being—as we say—realistic. "What time is it?" asks Norman Brown. And he answers: "Closing time." Let's face it: the times are apocalyptic.

But *facing* also means "putting a face on something," giving it form and figure, image and shape, so that we know what it is we are "facing," what we are up against: naming it, imagining it, like Adam with the animals.

This two-fold meaning seems to say that unless you imagine something, giving it a face, you cannot participate in it realistically, and therefore will not be facing it. It seems to imply that, in order to be literal, one has also to be poetic. And at the same time.

But the double-sally is itself doubled. Not only does *facing* have two senses, but also the word *apocalypse* is similarly duplex. We all know, not only from the film *Apocalypse Now,* but also from our own lives, that an "apocalypse" is the literal "end," the real Armageddon, finished and done for.

But the Greek word—we know too, even if we cannot understand it—means "revelation," "dis-closure" rather than merely closure. *Apo-calyptein* means "to un-cover," especially as in dream or vision, like the lifting of the veil for Ezekiel or John, writer of the Book of Revelation.

So, like the word *facing* in our theme, the term *apocalypse* is freighted with paradox: both literal and non-literal, history's end and religion's vision, as if the two were somehow and sometimes one. As the reigning apocalyptic theologian, Thomas J. J. Altizer, would say: apocalypse is dialectical, or it is not yet apocalyptic enough.

It may not be so easy, during our time together, to stay with this paradox and its dialectic, to stick with a paradoxical sensibility. But it is precisely the invitation to abide there, dwelling in the doubleness, "resting in the riddle" (Giradoux), residing in between the meanings, living in the irony, that has been extended to us who are here participant. To fall over, like Alice's White Knight or Luther's Drunken Sailor, into one side or the other—into some secure sense of revelation, opinion, truth, insight, or knowledge, on the one hand, or on the other into some sense of hopelessness, end, failure, or nihilism—will be to fail to entertain the idea under whose auspices we are being here entertained. To lose the paradox would mean that we have not "faced apocalypse."

We are therefore grateful in advance to our hostesses and hosts, those who have invited us to this experiment, so urgent in our history and crucial to our imagination, an experiment that from the outset is fated to make us humble.[1]

The Hartford insurance man and poet, Wallace Stevens, once wrote that "the steeples are empty and so are the people," thereby demonstrating his relevance to our apocalyptic topic. He also quipped, "thought is an infection," adding that "in the case of certain thoughts it becomes an epidemic."

Is not our time suffering from an epidemic, infected as it is with thoughts of the "end"? And are we not at this conference because we, too, are contaminated, having the Kierkegaardian "sickness unto death"?

The *thought* which sickens us today comes from former times of apocalypse, as well as from our own, even though our particular situation may be unique. Was there ever a time not apocalyptic for that age's sensitive and sick souls? The thought was already disclosed to Koheleth the Preacher, whose work in ancient Israel has come to be known, wrongly of course, as Ecclesiastes. In chapter seven, verse eight, of his book we read: "The end of a thing is better than its beginning."

Are we now anxious concerning persons in our midst who take this saying of Scripture literally? Or are we worrying our own inability to take it literally? Or, still further, are we unable today to say which of these is the case with us, not knowing our own dis-ease?

Whatever . . . *thoughts* about the "end" which sicken us are, as this biblical witness shows, at base and bottom *religious* thoughts. We suffer, all the more because unwittingly, from theology.[2]

Last December, in New York City, Professor Gordon Kaufman, a theologian from Harvard University, addressed the American Academy of Religion as its president, saying:

> All of us engaged in the study of religion are well aware that humankind has long contemplated the possibility of its ultimate extinction. Western religious traditions, for example, have been informed by the expectation of a final judgment by God in which the wheat will be separated from the chaff and all that is in opposition to God's purposes will be destroyed in a fiery holocaust as God brings his purposes to their ultimate consummation. The historicist world-view—which developed in ancient Israel, was appropriated and universalized by the Christian movement, and eventually became decisive in shaping modern western consciousness—easily lent itself to an exaggerated consciousness of futurity, and thus it was a natural matrix for the emergence of eschatological ideas. Though some always hoped that the consummation of history would be beneficent and healing of humanity's ills—at least for the faithful—others, like the prophet Amos, seemingly saw nothing but utter destruction in that final future. Jesus preaching . . . was informed throughout by the expectation of an imminent catastrophic ending of history, and there have been many Christian movements in the past two thousand years which picked up this strong eschatological consciousness, and looked forward to the return of the Lord on the clouds of heaven virtually momentarily. Thus the idea of a catastrophic end to history is "old stuff" for western religious and cultural traditions. . . . Surely those . . . teaching in the

field of religion studies might well think the prospect of a nuclear holocaust put us on quite familiar ground.

Kaufman seems to suggest that we might turn to the images of religions' histories to help us "face apocalypse," in whatever sense this phrase may have.

However, the apocalyptic vision in religion, traditional though it may be, "has been largely suppressed . . . since the Enlightenment," except in the minds of crazies, a fact which Kaufman himself admits. The vision *as vision* has been repressed. So, it would seem, we now have to live it out in life, literally. It is as if, when we lack a vision of the literal, we literalize unconscious vision. Is not the testimony universal? "Without a vision, the people perish."

Perhaps I, a theologian, have been invited here, to this conference, with the thought that it might be better to face the deep and perduring apocalyptic visions of our now unconscious traditions, those myths that have been long forgotten in our literalistic time, in order once again to make them conscious, in the possibility that theology could be a sort of therapy, making the unconscious conscious, leading back to vision our actings-out, giving face to what we have to face.[3]

But I, like Kaufman, am an odd sort of theologian. He was raised a Mennonite, and I was brought up in the Church of the Brethren. Our traditions, his and mine, are pietistic, from the left-wing of the so-called Reformation, related to the Amish and the German Baptist River Brethren, to which General Dwight David Eisenhower's Kansas grandmother belonged, but not he. We pietists are a bit out of step, neither Catholic nor really Protestant, standing between the two, distrusting one just as much as the other, operating from a "hermeneutic of suspicion" long before Paul Ricoeur invented the phrase to describe Nietzsche, Freud, and Marx.

Paranoia is the style of our left-wing religiosity—"in but not of the world," including the world of institutional religion. Ours is *ecclesiola in ecclesia,* a subversive group within the group, hating Calvin as much as Luther, and both as much as Popery and Papism; despising the State and its Germanic Princes as much as we dislike the Church. We were persecuted and martyred by both

Church and State; both were, to us, equally repressive. My father was a pacifist and conscientious objector during the Second World War, before it was trendy to engage in civil disobedience and before conferences such as this one could be announced in public.

"Despised, rejected, acquainted with grief"—we always believed more in action than in belief. At Hälle in Germany, in the eighteenth century, my people founded a community, building first a school and then a brewery, and only third a church. We practice Feet Washing during Holy Communion and serve an Agape Love Feast during the Eucharist in order to celebrate the eros of the Brethren and the Sisters, dipping real hand-baked bread in fresh beef broth. We anoint the sick for healing, not just the dying, and we—with Mennonites and Quakers—are one of only three historic peace churches in all of Christendom. Troeltsch called us "sect," not "church."

Above all, we distrust theology and theologians. We hate the creeds and seldom say them, taking instead, as we like to say, "the New Testament as our rule of faith and practice," by which we really mean the Gospels and not Paul, of whom we are also not so fond.

There is no mumbo-jumbo magic in our worship. Our people tend to be practical rather than spiritualist, like Pennsylvania Dutch farmers. We do not baptize babies. We let them make up their own minds when they are able. We are a voluntary association.

No bishops tell us what to do or say. We did not even pay our preachers at first and still under-pay them, just to make the point. Each congregation is autonomous. We like things differentiated, individualized, pluralistic but concrete, the body on the line, personally connected, but not connected to Church or State, connected rather to the pathos of every day's life.

We will not take an oath in court. When I was a child, my mother, like many of our women, wore a prayer covering during worship to protect against sexual attack, not only from mortal men, but also and especially, as the Bible says, from angels who get too close. We do not *like* hardly anyone; rather, our first principle is love, a *love* not taken personally and personalistically.

So, is it so surprising that we, like pietists everywhere and in whatever guise, are given to chiliasm? The personalistic and historicistic world is one in which we are not much at home, and we have a sense that others are not so at home in this literal egoic world either. So we tend to get happy when we sense an ending. The evening news of television almost tempts us to cheerfulness. We understand the crazy Millerites who went out on a hillside and waited for the end.

But why do I mention all this, and in so much detail? Because detail is what we need when "facing apocalypse" and because I have a hunch, a hunch that I intend here to labor a bit today, that the chiliastic vision from religion, this perduring transpersonal image and its complex, may be a bit of help now in the "facing of apocalypse."

Is it not the case that those who "face apocalypse" feel somehow different from those who repressively refuse, separate from those who do not seem to sense the imminence of the end? And is it not they who "face apocalypse," these pietists of whatever stripe, who tend toward chiliasm and worry much about being saved from extinction? Could it be that this is a conference, a "voluntary association," in which we are, perhaps unwillingly and unwittingly, a little like the chiliasts of pietistic religiosity, albeit here of course in secular mode.

What is this thing called "chiliasm"?[4]

It is an old, old story, and at first the matter is quite simple, though later it will become complex, what we shall come to call "the chiliast complex." *Chilias* means "one thousand" in Greek. For example, at the end of book eight of the *Iliad*, we may read:

Such in their numbers blazed the watchfires the Trojans were burning
between the waters of Xanthos and the ships, before Ilion.
A *thousand* fires were burning there in the plain, and beside each
one sat fifty men in the flare of the blazing firelight.
And standing each beside his chariot, champing white barley
and oats, the horses waited for the dawn to mount to her high place.

Similarly, in Aeschylus's play *The Persians,* a herald reports to the queen about the war:

Had number counted,
The barbarian warships surely would have won;

> The Greeks but numbered thirty tens, and ten
> Apart from these a chosen squadron formed;
> But Xerxes, and this I know full well, a *thousand*
> Led; and seven and two hundred ranked
> As queens in swiftness. The count stood so.
> Seemed we unequal? Some deity destroyed
> Our host, who weighing down the balance swung
> The beam of fortune. The gods saved the city
> Of the goddess.

Chilias, the word, has to do with numbers and with counting, but note well that in each of these instances the Greeks, favored by the Gods, were saved in spite of the "one thousand." This "being saved" is part and parcel of the fantasy of chiliasm, and it is already alive and well in very ancient Greece.

Plato, a little later, but still half a millennium before the Christian Apocalypse of St. John, added an association to the word *chilias.* Upping the ante to nine thousand in his dialogue *Phaedrus,* he made the term refer to the journey in the life to come. The person who refuses a life of philosophy, with its passion and erotic madness, will be destined, as Plato tells us, "to float for 9000 years around the earth and beneath it."

Plato amplifies his millennial point at the end of another work, the *Republic,* in a mythic tale of Er, son of Armenius. This man, or so the story goes, died and lay two days before burial on the funeral pyre. Just before the burning, he came back to life briefly, and he told what he had seen, namely, the company of souls from above and below, talking with one another, telling of their respective fates. The text reads:

> And they told their stories to one another, the ones lamenting and crying, remembering how much and what sort of things they had suffered and seen in the journey under the earth—*the journey that lasts a thousand years*—and those from heaven, in their turn, told of the inconceivable beauty of the experiences and the sights there.

So, the fantasy carried by the word *chilias,* half a millennium before the Christian movement, included in its complex the motifs of a miraculous salvation of "our people," a war going on, counting, death, and living in and after the end. Nor are the instances I have given isolated ones; to the contrary, in ancient Hellas they are not at all atypical.

Yet the term *chilias* fell into disuse in the Greek world. It is manifestly absent from papyri of the Hellenistic and Roman periods, with but a single exception that scholars can find (*P. Oxy.*, 16; seventh century C.E.). However, the term in no way died completely, any more than did the fantasy carried in its complex. A Jewish context nurtured both term and notion—in its own way, of course.[5]

Chilias and its cognates appear more than 250 times in the Septuagint (LXX), the Greek translation of Hebrew Scriptures, where this word renders the Hebrew *'eleph,* meaning "one thousand." The Greek term is common in Jewish Scripture, for example, in lists of numbers, as in this tabulation taken from a tally of the twelve tribes:

> Of the people of Judah, their generations, by their families, by their fathers' houses, according to the number of names, from twenty years old and upward, every man able to go forth to war: the number of the tribe of Judah was seventy-four *thousand* six hundred. (Num. 1: 26f., LXX)

The term is also commonly used, as it had also been in ancient Greece, when one wished to speak of a large number, even one beyond computation:

> A stream of fire issued and came forth from before him; a *thousand thousands* served him, and ten *thousand* times ten *thousand* stood before him; the court sat in judgment, and the books were opened. (Dan. 7: 10, LXX)

It would seem that when it is a question of "judgment," of whether or not I and my people "count," then counting happens, as if questions of quality petition answers of quantity—counting my good deeds, counting my beads, counting my blessings, counting my days. Do I "count"?

This fantasy of judging by calculation particularly arises in

Jewish contexts of old when the end is felt to be imminent, when there is an imminent sense of an ending of one sort or another. So, the Greek word *chilias* is often found in texts of Jewish apocalypse when there is speculation about the Messianic Age and its Great Banquet.

For example, the Ethiopian Enoch (14: 22) repeats the vision of Daniel when describing the Great Day in the Morning, and the Syrian Apocalypse of Baruch, which drew heavily on IV Esdras, anticipates imaginatively that in the Messianic Age each vine will have a *thousand* shoots, each shoot a *thousand* clusters, each cluster a *thousand* grapes, and each grape will produce a whole kor of wine (29: 5). But in the main, in these texts, the speculations have to do with time. How much time do we have? How much time will there be after the apocalyptic moment? And so on.

For example, in the Slavic Enoch (33: 1), the coming eighth millennium is the beginning of a new dispensation, while the 7000 years which have preceded it denote the seven days of a cosmic week, where each day is a *thousand* years. It was taught in the school of Elias that the world would last 6000 years, 2000 without the Torah, 2000 with the Torah, and 2000 with a Messiah. This school flourished during the Babylonian Captivity when the end seemed near for Israel. Indeed, down through the years, there have been many calculations by scribes concerning the length of the Messianic Age. Some said 2000 years, some said 7000 years, but it was most common to say 1000.

There was much debate among the Jews about this 1000-year period. It was clear that it was to be *an intermediate period*—which we may be in already—an intermediate time between historical existence as we knew it before and an end which is yet to come, a time which will give rise to the reign of God (viz., Ethiopian Enoch 91: 21f.; 93: 1–14; the Sybiline Oracles 3: 652–60; IV Esdras 7: 28f.; the Syrian Apocalypse of Baruch 29: 3; 30: 1–5; 40: 3). But the question is debated: When will a savior-messiah and our salvation come in relation to when the end occurs? Will there be salvation before the end? or only after?

According to the older of two views, the Messiah, who is yet to come, will be an end-time King, restoring the monarchy of David and raising it to new heights. This was a nationalistic view. But there was also, and later, as the end seemed more imminent, a more universal sense. On this view, God's envoy would appear, and *all* who had previously died would be raised and be brought to judgment, as if we are all in this together.

These two views were, later still, fused. The reign of the Messiah-King would come before the end of the world, so that there would be an earthly Messianic Age, perhaps for one thousand years, and it would be followed by a last assault of the powers of chaos prior to the commencement of a future and completely different world.

Now this may all seem a little silly and abstractly speculative, confirming Michelet's view that "theology is the art of befuddling oneself methodically." But it may be well to keep this old warring dialectic close to memory, for the fight was to rage again in Christian circles, especially those which were pietistic, where individuals were made to declare whether they were pre-millennialist or post-millennialist, whether they imagined that their Savior would come before the thousand years or at the thousand years' end. It is a perduring problematic fantasy, even if one we now repress, projecting it onto a fanatic fringe. If we could face this fantasy, it might well serve as image for our own secular and modern sense in the face of imagined end, ecological and political.

But already we move too quickly. There is yet another chapter to the chiliast story. Even two more.[6]

So far we have seen that the apocalyptic fantasia, its complex of images, is the offspring of a wedding of Jew and Greek, not to mention the nudge this shotgun marriage received under pressures of chaotic political times from Persian and Gnostic matchmakers. The motifs were already in place: a sense of an end, feeling a raging warfare, a dying of Jewish and Hellenic traditions, and, in the face and facing of this, counting on whether I "count," worrying the judgment of *all* (that is, the saving or extinction of everyone) in relation to the salvation of *a few* (that is, the notion that some will remain), anxious about timing (that is, where I fit into the times and in time itself).

These themes, together with the heavy sense that "the time is near to hand," were present in the person of the Christian John, when the Emperor Domitian brought about his personal "end," exiling him politically for his religious protest to the island of Patmos, where he had a vision which became, not only a wedding of disparate pasts—Jew and Greek—but also a dream for all chiliasts of the future. He dreamed our complex.

For our purposes here, tracing the chiliast story, the twentieth chapter of the Apocalypse of St. John, the Book of Revelation, is most relevant. In this chapter, the word *chilias* serves to bring to dream-expression, like some collective, condensing *Tagesreste,* the re-visioning of Jewish apocalyptic and Greek rhetoric. John reports the scene this way:

> Then I saw an angel coming down from heaven, holding in his hand the key of the bottomless pit and a great chain. And he seized the dragon, that ancient serpent, who is the Devil and Satan, and bound him for a *thousand* years, and threw him into the pit, and shut it and sealed it over him, that he should deceive the nations no more, till the *thousand* years were ended. After that he must be loosed for a little while. (Rev. 20: 1–3)

Then John goes on to describe the "thrones" and the "souls" gathered about the seat of "judgment," not so unlike the descriptions of Daniel and Baruch. The souls who have died, suffering the end-time, dwell with Christ during the thousand-year interregnum. Then:

> . . . when the *thousand* years are ended, Satan will be loosed from his prison and will come out to deceive the nations which are at the four corners of the earth . . . to gather them for battle; their number is like the sand of the sea. (Rev. 20: 7–8)

This final conflict will function, according to John's imagination, to produce something entirely different: "a new heaven and a new earth; for the first heaven and the first earth had passed away, and the sea was no more" (Rev. 21: 1).

The vision and its imagery seem clear enough on the face of it. But what is also clear is that John's Apocalypse, the Book of Revelation, has been unclear to everyone from the beginning. So, there has been a clear-cut case of repression, as Domitian repressed its author. It has remained untold, unstudied, and hence unconscious as vision, scripture, myth, and dream. And so we today gather, two millennia later, "facing apocalypse," not as vision and scripture, not as myth and dream, but as acting-out, literally lived, imminent "sense of an ending," really and not merely literary trope, explained by Frank Kermode.

John's vision concerning our situation could be suggestive. It implies that, when we have a sense of an ending, our sense places us in a "between"—between something that is dying or dead and another something that has yet to be dis-closed, between already and not yet. This *between* is called *chilias*, "one thousand"; yet like the Hebrew *'eleph*, it also means "much," "many," "so many as to be incalculable." *Chilias* is counting the uncountable. So many persons; so many years. The time of being "in the middle" is incalculable because it is so great. And when things are incalculable—1000, 2000, 7000 megaton bombs—then we are, willy nilly, *chiliasts*, in the middle, between a rock and a hard place, neither here nor there, and it'll probably last a "thousand" years!

Each motif in the fantasy evokes the others. Chiliasm is an apocalyptic complex. "When something seems to be ended or ending, a war seems to be going on." "This warring may contain finality." "Will anything be saved?" "Do I count?" "There is no way to calculate what's happening." "And when there is no way to calculate what's happening, it must be the end." "Times are tough, so we must count the days till the end." "And when we count the days, worrying time, the times, and timing, then things get tough." "Nothing from before is to the point, and whatever is next to be must be completely different." "People don't understand." "They think I'm crazy." "People won't listen." "And this proves that things are ending." . . . so sings the chiliast complex.

Surely we all know all too well this apocalyptic fantasy, its reality, for we are chiliasts all, were we to face it—in the face of, say, leaving home, planning suicide, divorce, the death of one beloved, loss of money or job, Nazi holocaust, ecological crisis, nuclear threat. And, of course, this is not the whole laundry list of what we face, not the end; it's only the beginning. No wonder the face of chiliasm is repressed, in both self and in society.[7]

Though John's vision, like he himself, was despised and rejected, shunned and repressed (apocalypse refusing to be faced), there have always been, here and there, those for whom chapter twenty of the Book of Revelation was the crux of life's meaning, just as, for all of us, now and then, its fantasy is crucial. Victor Turner called these chiliasts "liminal," meaning that they are "on the boundary," "marginal," "between." He likened their situation in the Western social tradition to bohemians, court jesters, monastics, and third-world nations. Feeling neither here nor there, they are, as Turner put it, "betwixt and between." A litany of their names (not all, to be sure) will serve to make the point—the point being made because we know so little of them.

There were: Lactantius (third century), Adso of Montior-en-Der (tenth century), Joachim of Fiore (twelfth century), Angelo of Clareno and Peter John Olivi (thirteenth century), and Savonarola (fifteenth century), who was attacked by Marsilio Ficino as being the Anti-Christ—Ficino thereby showing his own chiliastic sense.

On the continent of Europe, also in the fifteenth century, there were the Hussites, followed by the Anabaptists (sixteenth century) and the pietistic Bohemian Brotherhood (seventeenth century). In Great Britain, in the eighteenth and nineteenth centuries, there were the Diggers, the Albury Group, John Ward, and the Southcottians. In the United States, during the last two centuries, there have been the Millerites, Seventh Day Adventists, Mormons, Jehovah's Witnesses, and the Friends of the Eternal. But this is not yet representative, for chiliasm is not limited to Christianity.

In Jewish circles there were Rabbi Johanan ben Zakkai and his little group, then Rabbi Akiba, not to mention all that is contained in *hekaloth* literature, so well traced by Gershom Scholem. In Islam it was standard belief that a Mahdi would come to usher in the New Age and that he, with the prophet Jesus, would rule the interregnum and die naturally, like Jesus, just before the End. The Nizārī Ismāʻīlīs, also called "Assassins," at one time believed that the Mahdi had already come and that we are now in the thousand-year period, but that it is to be interpreted as a timeless state of mind. Nor have we yet mentioned the Nativistic Cargo Cults, the Ras Tafarians and Rock Music. (Have you noticed how rock music today, obsessed with apocalypse as it is in its lyrics, has no actual endings in its music, simply fading off—no bang, just whimper!) And, there is Christopher Columbus, too! In his account of "The Fourth Voyage," in a letter by him called *Lettera Rarissima,* the voyager told his vision, how his divinely inspired mission would open a path to a New World, heralding an age of universal conversion, which would precede by just a bit the End of the World. America was, so to say, "discovered" by a chiliast!

There has, of course, been no end to counting among these people who, chiliastically speaking, "count." Justin Martyr, who lived in the second century, expected the end, as he said, "soon." Hippolytus imagined it would come a little later, in 500 C.E., and Augustine put the date at 1000. Because of the 1260 days mentioned in John's Apocalypse (12: 6), the year 1260 was a favorite. Others made other calculations concerning the incalculable: 1365, 1367, 1660, 1688, 1689, 1715, 1730, 1734, 1774. In 1827 the Plymouth Brethren said it would happen any day. The Mormons, Latter Day Saints, began their predictions in 1830. They were followed by William Miller who picked 1834, and then 1844, and then gave up counting. But the Seventh Day Adventist movement continued his number business. Nor need I say here that since the two World Wars, numerous others have joined the counting: 1984, 2000, 2001, and so on.

The point to this recital of names and ever-pressing final dates is to note yet another motif crucial to the chiliast complex: *literalism*. The new Roman Catholic encyclopedia of theology, *Sacramentum Mundi,* says that "the symbolic interpretation of Revelation prevailed in the Church . . . but there were repeated efforts to understand the text as a prophecy of concrete events." These are of course the chiliasts, whose attempts are repeated in the face of an orthodox Christian refusal to face apocalypse, symbolizing it with theological sleight-of-tongue. Such refusal produces a form of literalism that is repugnant beyond belief, as has been recently demonstrated in an article in the *Boston Globe,* May 2, 1982, section A, page 1. There one can find a report on a group of modern chiliasts, whose literalism is as incredible as the Church's seemingly opposite orthodox denial. They assert that any who oppose the nuclear arms race are in fact guilty of opposing God's will, since they would be standing in the way of the End, which, in their fancy, would be an expression of the purpose of God!

Perverse as this may be, and it is surely most perverse, the association of a sense of the end with moralistic literalism is perennial. It was already prepared in a pun well-practiced in ancient Greece. The philosophers then often explained the Greek word *telos,* meaning "end," by linking it to the word for "perfection," *teleios* (viz., Aristotle, *Metaphysics* 4.16, 1021b; Plato, *Cratylus* 403e, and *Laws* 2.653a). Aquinas, too, wrote: *"Perfectio consistit in hoc quod pertingat ad finem"* (Perfection consists in that which extends toward an end—*De nom* 1.3). It is a recurring sense, this image of linking ending to literal action, and it is something we have to face in the thousand faces of our own chiliasms.

Does this sound familiar? When we sense an imminent end, the ending of anything, or everything, we tend toward literalism and action, wondering what we can *do* while waiting for the end, anxious to be one of the responsible ones, the good ones, the "chosen" ones, and wondering if the saving moment will come before the end or after it, thereby raising, like all good chiliasts, the question of pre- or post-millennialism. Or, to put it differently: in those moments when we in life go literal—in relationship, in vocation, in relation to despair about ourselves or nation, in ecological or political situation—do we not then wonder about the end, the dying, the liminality of our lives and psyches?

Just here lies a problem. Becoming literal, fundamentalistic in a thousand ways, we begin to lose the paradox, the dialectic, the irony. We swing to one side or the other, no longer between, hastening the Day of Judgment by ourselves judging and by judging ourselves.

The chiliast paradox—in ancient Greece and Israel, in John's dream-vision and Western chiliast history—is that literal and metaphoric belong together. And the proper dialectic of this paradox involves a movement from literal to mythic, *not the reverse.* The chiliast first senses a literal end in the social chaos, and she or he places that sense, that ending-scenario, that script, in scripture, in a dream, a vision, a mythical account, knowing that fantasies of the end are transpersonal, archetypal, fundamentally religious.

The strategy is to seek images of the literal while giving literal action to imagination's life, as part of the imagining. It is as if, dialectically, literalism is one of the figures of speech, one of the myths, one of the metaphors—literalism as one of the perspectives through which we view our world and life.[8]

We all need images of the literal, ways to imagine what is happening when we go literal, as inevitably we will do, from time to time, having sensed some potential end. At those moments, can there be living spirit *in* dead letter? Not saved *from* dead letter, but *in* it. Can we see meaning in the fundamentals, see images in our own fundamentalisms, in those times and places that we all go literal? Do we not, in our time especially—a time of Reagan, of Egonomics, of Jerry Falwell, of everything and everybody moving to the right—need ways of understanding the literal, rather than refusing to face it? When the times seem apocalyptic, literalism sets in; and, when literalism sets in, the times will surely seem apocalyptic, at least to some of us.

The literal is one of the Gods of our eternal pantheon, one of the Immortals, archetypal image connected with apocalyptic sense. It keeps showing up in life. Indeed, we will be, now and then, at the end, stuck, between the Devil and the Deep Blue Sea. But if we have images for our stuckness—faces—then we may be able to face it, thereby being not so stuck in our very stucknesses and, above all, not leaving literalism and the business of the end to those amongst us who take their literalisms literally, in religion and in politics.

Literal: our word comes from the Latin *littera,* which the authorities, Lewis and Short, say means "a letter," and they say it comes from *lino,* an active verb meaning "to daub," "to smear," "to spread or rub over," from the Sanskrit root *li-,* meaning "to let go" and "to pour," by way of the Greek *leibō,* meaning "to pour forth"—as *oinon leibein,* "to pour forth wine" (in *Iliad* 1.463 and *Odyssey* 3.460) and especially *Dii leibein oinon,* "to pour forth a libation to the gods" (in *Iliad* 7.481 and *Odyssey* 2.432). From thence we get *littera,* our "letter" and "literals" being a libation of a divine sort, but our literalisms also being *limus,* meaning "slime," "mud," "mire," and "shit." Dialectic intact!

Fine. But Lewis and Short are out of academic style. The insight of their important linguistic fantasy—namely, that our literalist shit can be a libation and that it properly belongs to the Gods—is based, as is nowadays said, on false etymology. The *Oxford English Dictionary (OED)* and Eric Partridge tell us the so-called literal truth, but one which carries no fantasy of the literal with it: namely, "the once popular relationship to L *linere,* to smear, pp *litus,* is largely discredited" (Partridge); "of obscure origin—the hypothesis that it is connected with *linere,* to smear, is now generally rejected" (*OED*).

Score this philological anecdote as representative of our condition in these latter days, lacking images for our literalism, leaving literalism thereby in the hands of the literalists, to the fundamentalists of Church and State. The shit is repressed, and the Gods have gone. We have no history, no story, no source, no image, no perspective for those times when we go literal. We no longer know what we do, or what to do, when we sense an ending imminent. We cannot remember on what God to pour out our shit. Our letters are dead letters, having no spirit in them.

But this has been my very point today: *that religion's crazy chiliasm is at least one archetypal image of literalism!* Is it not the case that chiliasm's story shows us components of our apocalyptic complex? Is not its fantasia a perspective, a way of seeing and sensing our sense of ending? Does it not already notice that the literal is one way of being in the world, a myth, myth of the literal, where the literal is not so stuck in and on itself, as is the case of American politics (the State) and American religious fundamentalism (the Church). In the *mythos* of chiliasm, literalism has a story, a history, imagery, and depth; indeed, it has a dialectic that is not opposite to metaphor and myth, but is well-lettered. Chiliasm can teach us about our literalisms, helping us (as Norman Brown has said) to "re-learn our letters" and (as Denise Levertov has written) to "re-learn the alphabet." Chiliasm's optic is a way of seeing the fantasy in our behavior and our behaviorism, thereby helping us to note (as James Hillman urges) that behavior is fantasy, too, and always.

Literalism is thus released, and we are released to act, to be literal. For in chiliasm our protests, our paranoias, our fears, our civil and not-so-civil obedience and disobedience are transpersonalized. Action is placed in vision without losing its activity. Metaphor and literal are in dialectic, neither being bottom line for the other. Apocalypse is faced, because in chiliasm one has at least one face for apocalypse. The literal, then, is one of our lively metaphors, like the filming by Marxist-Atheist director Emilio de Antonio of the protest by the Berrigans and others of the Ploughshares 8, at the G. E. nuclear plant: "In the King of Prussia."

William Stringfellow observed that in this film political action, because imagined, has achieved liturgical and ritual meaning.[9]

Chiliasm knows a thing or two. It knows that when we face apocalypse literally, sensing some end imminent, imagination begins. In the face of endings, not only do we go crazy like the chiliasts, but also like them we imagine things. Apocalypse ("end") makes apocalypse ("revelation"). Closure produces dis-closure, if we face it.

Indeed. When we face apocalypse, being literally realistic about our literal ends, the apocalypse we face receives some face, while we are waiting for the end. When we look at what we imagine to be literal, we may, once again, be able literally to imagine.

Fantasies of the end stop us dead, stop those who, in the Jewish-Christian-Islamic tradition of moving time and history, wish for things to move. Facing apocalypse brings dream, vision, nightmare imaginings of life's literalisms.

When we consider the end, we may be able to say: "I have a dream." Then our ending has some end, some point—and not just a single point.

The chiliastic dream of closure discloses a thousand faces—a thousand vine-branches, a thousand years in a single day, a thousand angel-voices, a thousand demons—not a single chosen group. We are all in this together, then and now, here and now, caught in the middle.

Chiliasm shows—and doubtless this is one reason why, in our wish for single-mindedness, it is repressed—apocalypse with a thousand faces, all souls, counting that which one can never count on. No end to it.[10]

David Miller has grouped references by section of his article. They are printed in order of their appearance.

1. Viz., Norman O. Brown, *Closing Time* (New York: Random House, 1973), and "Apocalypse: The Place of Mystery in the Life of the Mind"; S. R. Hopper and D. L. Miller, eds., *Interpretation: The Poetry of Meaning* (New York: Harcourt, Brace, and World, 1967); Thomas J. J. Altizer, *The New Apocalypse: The Radical Christian Vision of William Blake* (n.p.: Michigan State University Press, 1967), *The Descent into Hell: A Study of the Radical Reversal of the Christian Consciousness* (New York: Crossroad, 1979), and "The

Apocalyptic Identity of the Modern Imagination"; C. Winquist, ed., *The Archaeology of the Imagination* (Chico, California: American Academy of Religion, 1981), pp. 19–30.

2. Wallace Stevens, "Loneliness in Jersey City," in *Collected Poems* (New York: Alfred A. Knopf, 1954), p. 210, and "Adagia," in *Opus Posthumous* (New York: Alfred A. Knopf, 1977), p. 158.

3. Gordon D. Kaufman, "Nuclear Eschatology and the Study of Religion," *Journal of the American Academy of Religion* 51/1 (March 1983): 3–4.

4. Paul Ricoeur, *Freud and Philosophy: An Essay on Interpretation* (New Haven: Yale University Press, 1970), pp. 32 ff. and pass. Viz., William M. Beahm, *Studies in Christian Belief* (Elgin: The Brethren Press, 1958), especially chap. 14, and Dale Aukerman, *Darkening Valley: A Biblical Perspective on Nuclear War* (New York: The Seabury Press, 1981). Both of these books, by Beahm and Aukerman, are typical statements by writers from the Church of the Brethren.

5. *Iliad* 8.560–65; Aeschylus, *The Persians,* 338–48; Plato, *Phaedrus,* 275a, and *The Republic,* 615a. Viz., Gerhard Friedrich, ed., G. W. Bromiley, trans., *Theological Dictionary of the New Testament* (Grand Rapids: Eerdmans Publishing Co., 1974), 9: 466–71 (*"chilias, chilioi"*); and John J. Collins, ed., *Apocalypse: The Morphology of a Genre, Semeia 14* (Chico, California: Society of Biblical Literature, 1979).

6. Viz., Christopher Rowland, *The Open Heaven: A Study of Apocalyptic in Judaism and Early Christianity* (New York: Crossroad, 1982); Friedrich, *Theological Dictionary;* and Collins, *Apocalypse.*

7. Viz., Gilles Quispel, *The Secret Book of Revelation: The Last Book of the Bible* (New York: McGraw-Hill Book Co., 1979).

8. Victor Turner, "Liminality and Communitas," in *The Ritual Process: Structure and Anti-Structure* (Chicago: Aldine Publishing Co., 1969), and "Betwixt and Between: The Liminal Period in Rites of Passage," in *The Forest of Symbols* (Ithaca: Cornell University Press, 1967), pp. 93–111; Karl Rahner et al., eds., *Sacramentum Mundi: An Encyclopedia of Theology* (New York: Herder and Herder, 1969), 4: 43 f. ("Millenarianism"). Viz., Amos Wilder, "The Rhetoric of Ancient and Modern Apocalyptic," *Interpretation* 25 (1971): 436–53; Norman Cohn, *The Pursuit of the Millennium* (New York: Harper & Row, 1961); Bernard McGinn, *Visions of the End: Apocalyptic Traditions in the Middle Ages* (New York: Columbia University Press, 1979); Bernard McGinn and Marjorie Reeves, *Apocalyptic Spirituality* (New York: Paulist Press, 1979); John A. T. Robinson, *In the End God* (New York: Harper & Row, 1968); W. H. Oliver, *Prophets and Millennialists* (n.p.: Oxford University Press, 1978); Sylvia Thrupp, ed., *Millennial Dreams in Action: Essays in Comparative Study* (The Hague: Mouton and Co., 1962); Michael Barkun, *Disaster and the Millennium* (New Haven: Yale University Press, 1974); and Beahm, *Studies in Christian Belief,* pp. 258–62.

9. C. T. Lewis and C. C. Short, eds., *A Latin Dictionary* (Oxford: Clarendon Press, 1879), s.v. *"littera"*; Eric Partridge, *Origins: A Short Etymological*

Dictionary of Modern English (New York: The Macmillan Co., 1958), s.v. "literal"; *The Compact Edition of the Oxford English Dictionary* (New York: Oxford University Press, 1971), s.v. "literal"; Norman O. Brown, *Closing Time,* p. 104; Denise Levertov, *Relearning the Alphabet* (New York: New Directions, 1970); James Hillman, "An Essay on Pan," in *Pan and the Nightmare* (Dallas: Spring Publications, 1972), p. xxxix.

10. Viz., Patricia Berry, "Stopping: A Mode of Animation," in *Echo's Subtle Body* (Dallas: Spring Publications, 1982), pp. 147–62; Frank Kermode, *The Sense of an Ending* (New York: Oxford University Press, 1967); Stanley Romaine Hopper, "The Relationship of Religion to Art and Culture: The Mythologies of Collapse" (Mimeographed version of lecture delivered at the Chautauqua Institution, summer 1974); David L. Miller, "Images of Happy Ending," in *Eranos Yearbook 44–1975* (Leiden: E. J. Brill, 1977), pp. 61–89, and "Imaginings No End," in *Eranos Yearbook 46–1977* (Frankfurt: Insel Verlag, 1981), pp. 451–99.

ROBERT JAY LIFTON

The first to study the psychological effects of the nuclear threat, psychiatrist Robert Jay Lifton was among the pioneer investigators at Hiroshima and Nagasaki. Born in Brooklyn in 1926, Dr. Lifton is now Foundations' Fund Research Professor of Psychiatry at Yale School of Medicine. His prolific writings include the award-winning *Death in Life: Survivors of Hiroshima, History and Human Survival,* and *Indefensible Weapons.* Dr. Lifton is also an active member of Physicians for Social Responsibility.

The Image of "The End of the World"
A Psychohistorical View

The question of end-of-the-world imagery takes us to the heart of
contemporary nuclear threat, psychological theory, and the relationship between the two. Conceptual and moral struggles merge
here, as old models are found wanting, and we grope for new
ones.

I want to begin with three sets of quotations: first, from
Hiroshima survivors; second, from a much smaller, little-known
disaster; and third, from a very famous psychiatric patient.

I. Hiroshima, Buffalo Creek, and Daniel Paul Schreber

When an atomic bomb was dropped over Hiroshima, the most
striking psychological feature of survivors' response was the immediate and absolute shift from normal existence to an overwhelming encounter with death. A shopkeeper's assistant conveys
this feeling rather characteristically, without explicit end-of-the-
world imagery but in a tone consistent with it:

> It came very suddenly. . . . I felt something like an electric—a
> bluish sparkling light. . . . There was a noise, and I felt great
> heat—even inside the house. . . . I didn't know anything about the
> atomic bomb so I thought that some bomb had fallen directly upon
> me. . . . And then when I felt that our house had been directly hit, I
> became furious. . . . There were roof tiles and walls—everything
> black—entirely covering me. So I screamed for help. . . . And from
> all around I heard moans and screaming, and then I felt a kind of

danger to myself. . . . I thought that I too was going to die in that way. I felt this way at that moment because I was absolutely unable to do anything at all by my own power. . . . I didn't know where I was or what I was under. . . . I couldn't hear voices of my family. I didn't know how I could be rescued. I felt I was going to suffocate and then die, without knowing exactly what happened to me. This was the kind of expectation I had. . . .[1]

Survivors recalled initial feelings related to death and dying, such as "This is the end for me" or "My first feeling was, 'I think I will die.'" But beyond those feelings was the sense that the whole world was dying. That sense was expressed by a physicist who was covered with debris and temporarily blinded: "My body seemed black, everything seemed dark, dark all over. . . . Then I thought, 'The world is ending.'"[2]

A Protestant minister, himself uninjured, but responding to the mutilation and destruction he saw everywhere around him, experienced his end-of-the-world imagery in an apocalyptic Christian idiom:

> The feeling I had was that everyone was dead. The whole city was destroyed. . . . I thought all of my family must be dead—it doesn't matter if I die. . . . I thought this was the end of Hiroshima—of Japan—of humankind. . . . This was God's judgment on man. . . .[3]

His memory is inseparable from his theology, in the sense that everyone's memory of such events is inseparable from fundamental interpretive principles.

A woman writer also remembered religious imagery, probably Buddhist:

> I just could not understand why our surroundings had changed so greatly in one instant. . . . I thought it might have been something which had nothing to do with the war, the collapse of the earth which it was said would take place at the end of the world, and which I had read about as a child. . . .[4]

This sense of world collapse could also be expressed symbolically, as in the immediate thought of a devoutly religious domestic worker: "There is no God, no Buddha."[5]

Some survivors called forth humor, inevitably "gallows humor," as a way of mocking their own helplessness and the absurdity of total destruction. A professional cremator, for instance, though severely burned, managed to make his way back to his home (adjoining the crematorium) and said that he felt relieved because "I thought I would die soon, and it would be convenient to have the crematorium close by."[6]

Many recollections convey the dream-like grotesqueness of the scene of the dead and the dying, and the aimless wandering of the living. All this was sensitively rendered by Dr. Michihiko Hachiya in his classic *Hiroshima Diary:*

> Those who were able walked silently toward the suburbs in the distant hills, their spirits broken, their initiative gone. When asked whence they had come, they pointed to the city and said "that way"; and when asked where they were going, pointed away from the city and said "this way." They were so broken and confused that they moved and behaved like automatons.
>
> Their reactions had astonished outsiders who reported with amazement the spectacle of long files of people holding stolidly to a narrow, rough path when close by was a smooth easy road going in the same direction. The outsiders could not grasp the fact that they were witnessing the exodus of a people who walked in the realm of dreams.[7]

People characterized those they saw in such strange states (near-naked, bleeding, faces disfigured and bloated from burns, arms held awkwardly away from the body to prevent friction with other burned areas), and by implication themselves, as being "like so many beggars" or "like . . . red Jizō [stone image of Buddhist deity] standing on the sides of the road." Above all, there was so great a sense of silence as to suggest the absence of all life. Again the woman writer: "It was quiet around us. . . . in fact there was a fearful silence which made one feel that all people and all trees and vegetation were dead. . . ."[8] Similarly, Dr. Hachiya was struck by the "uncanny stillness" permeating his hospital: ". . . one thing was common to everyone I saw—complete silence. . . . one spoke. . . . Why was everyone so quiet? . . . it was as though I walked through a gloomy, silent motion picture. . . ."[9]

In all this there was a profound disruption in the relationship between death and life. This confusion of distinction between one's sense of being alive or dead was conveyed by a grocer, himself severely burned:

> The appearance of people was . . . well, they all had skin blackened by burns. . . . They had no hair because their hair was burned, and at a glance you couldn't tell whether you were looking at them from in front or in back. . . . They held their arms bent [forward] like this [he proceeded to demonstrate their position] . . . and their skin— not only on their hands, but on their faces and bodies too—hung down. . . . If there had been only one or two such people . . . perhaps I would not have had such a strong impression. But wherever I walked I met these people. . . . Many of them died along the road—I can still picture them in my mind—like walking ghosts. . . . They didn't look like people of this world. . . . They had a special way of walking—very slowly. . . . I myself was one of them.[10]

Whatever life remained seemed unrelated to a natural order and more part of a supernatural or "unnatural" one. These impressions emerged in frequently expressed imagery of a Buddhist hell that seemed to provide an interpretation for understanding the immediate situation. A young sociologist's description:

> My immediate thought was that this was like the hell I had always read about. . . . I had never seen anything which resembled it before, but I thought that should there be a hell, this was it—the Buddhist hell, where we were taught that people who could not attain salvation always went. . . . And I imagined that all of these people I was seeing were in the hell that I had read about.[11]

These Hiroshima memories, then, combine explicit end-of-the-world imagery with a grotesque dream-like aura of a non-natural situation, a form of existence in which life was so permeated by death as to become virtually indistinguishable from it.

The small disaster at Buffalo Creek, West Virginia, in which I and others became involved, was a flood in which 125 people were killed and nearly 500 made homeless.[12] The flood, which occurred in 1972, resulted from massive corporate negligence in the form of dumping coal waste in a mountain stream in a manner that created an artificial dam, causing increasingly dangerous water pressure to build up behind it. After several days of rain, the dam gave way and a massive moving wall of "black water," more than thirty feet high, roared through the narrow creek hollow.

While interviewing survivors, I was struck by many resemblances to the patterns I found in Hiroshima. There was not, of course, the Hiroshima aura of ultimate destruction and merging of death and life. But as a "total disaster" in the sense of the complete destruction of a finite area, it produced its own end-of-the-world imagery. Memories of destruction became encompassing, with at least the momentary sense on the part of a number of survivors that "it was the end of time." In an analogous but much more limited way, Buffalo Creek survivors described the contrast between the hopeful movement of life existing prior to the disaster and the hopeless stagnation after it. As an incapacitated miner expressed it:

> It's a split decision. There's the life you lived before and the life you live after. Before the disaster it seemed like you got up and you looked forward; there was something I was going ahead to—the garden, the horses, the job. The garden is gone; there are trailers where the horses were; there's no job left.[13]

Memories of the disaster were still extremely vivid during interviews conducted thirty months after the flood. As one man interviewed in May 1974 put it: "Everything came to an end—just stopped. Everything was wiped out."[14]

The third set of quotations I want to present are from a gifted man's account of his disturbed mental state. Daniel Paul Schreber, a distinguished German judge, could hardly have realized in 1903, when he published his *Memoirs of My Nervous Illness* of a decade or so before, that he was providing psychoanalytic psychiatry with what was to become the celebrated Schreber "case." From those memoirs, Freud constructed a concept of schizophrenia, especially paranoid schizophrenia, that has informed, haunted, and confused psychiatric work on psychosis ever since.

Schreber's own account of his psychosis, extraordinarily articulate, can be a source of considerable insight to anyone who studies it carefully. One of the smaller ironies of subsequent German history lies in the fact that the place in which he had these experiences that were to contribute so much to human understanding, the asylum at Sonnenstein, was to become deeply implicated in the Nazi mass-murder of mental patients under the euphemism of "euthanasia" just a few decades later.

Schreber was preoccupied with the idea of a "world catastrophe," which he thought at times necessary for the re-creation of the species, and for the possibility of his (Schreber's) giving birth to children in the manner of a woman. In other words, world destruction and re-creation. In one passage he describes some of this delusional and hallucinatory system in connection with observations on the stars and mysterious cosmic events:

> When later I regularly visited the garden and again saw—my memory does not fully deceive me—two suns in the sky at the same time, one of which was our earthly sun. The other was said to be the Cassiopeian group of stars drawn together into a single sun. From the sum total of my recollections, my impression gained hold of me that the period in question, which according to human calculations stretched over three to four months, had covered an immensely long period. It was as if single nights had a duration of centuries. So that within that time the most profound alterations in the whole of mankind, and the earth itself, and the whole solar system might very well have taken place. It was repeatedly mentioned in visions that the work of the past 1400 years had been lost. . . .[15]

When Schreber says "repeatedly mentioned," he refers to his "visions" or hallucinations. He considers the figure of 1400 years to be an indication of "the duration of time that the earth has been populated" and remembers hearing another figure, about 200 or 212 years, for the time still "allotted to the earth."

> During the latter part of my stay in Flechsig's Asylum [Prof. Flechsig was the director] I thought this period had already expired and therefore I was the last real human being left, and that the few human shapes I saw apart from myself—Professor Flechsig, some attendants, occasional more or less strange-looking-patients, were only "fleeting-improvised-men" created by miracle. I pondered over

> such possibilities as that the whole of Flechsig's Asylum or perhaps
> the city of Leipzig with it had been "dug out" and moved to some
> other celestial body, all of them possibilities which questions asked
> by the voices who talked to me seemed to hint at, as for instance
> whether Leipzig was still standing, etc. I regarded the starry sky
> largely, if not wholly, extinguished.[16]

Here the world-catastrophe is accompanied by re-creation, with
Schreber himself at the center of it. Thus he goes on to speak of
seeing "beyond the walls of the Asylum only a narrow strip of
land," so strange and different that "at times one spoke of a holy
landscape."

> I lived for years in doubt as to whether I was really still on earth or
> whether on some other celestial body. . . . In the soul-language dur-
> ing [that] time . . . I was called *"the seer of spirits,"* that is, a man
> who sees, and is in communication with, spirits or departed souls.[17]

These quotations from Schreber convey the kind of end-of-the-
world imagery one encounters in acute and chronic forms of
psychosis, usually paranoid schizophrenic psychosis. We will have
more to say about schizophrenia and about Schreber, but here we
may note that the psychotic dies *with* the world, in that his sense of
inner disintegration includes self and world. But by rendering
himself at the same time the only survivor, he expresses the particular paranoid struggle with vitality and pseudo-vitality, and indeed a paranoid or distorted vision of regeneration. But as Freud
told us, the impulse toward restitution in symptoms of schizophrenia or symptoms of any kind is always present.

II. End-of-the-World Imagery and Levels of Experience

I have chosen these three groups of quotations because they say
something about a continuum that I believe exists in relation to
end-of-the-world imagery. On the one end of the continuum, we
find a more or less socially acceptable response to actual historical
events involving extreme destructiveness. At the other end is what
we consider a mental aberration or paranoid delusion. I emphasize
the continuum in order to suggest that, even at its extremes

—Hiroshima and schizophrenia—there are important relationships and even similarities in their end-of-the-world imagery.

Christian millennial images can, at least at times, be included among the relatively acceptable interpretations. That is true as long as the theological structure of meaning, the eschatology involving something like Armageddon, is generally believed. Considering actual historical events, that interpretation is more acceptable in connection with Hiroshima than Buffalo Creek, simply because of scale. Yet when it is realized that the latter completely destroyed a small community—inundating it with death, so to speak—imagery of world-ending associated with it becomes more understandable to an outside observer.

From this perspective, three levels of experience must be distinguished. There is first the external event, such as the Hiroshima bomb. We could also speak of the plagues of the Middle Ages as an external event, so much so that there were some notable similarities in imagery between plague survivors and survivors of Hiroshima.[18] Second, there is the shared theological imagery, or eschatology, that renders such imagery acceptable as a meaning structure. Finally, there is the internal derangement—the intrapsychic disintegration or personal Armageddon of psychosis, especially in certain schizophrenic syndromes.

These distinctions are necessary and even useful, but if maintained in an absolute sense they become a barrier to our understanding of this kind of imagery. So I pose them in order to suggest their limitations, in order to move beyond their either/or categories.

All three of the elements are, I believe, present in each of the three experiences we are considering. If we take Hiroshima, for instance, there is an overwhelming external event and there is an internal experience, something like internal breakdown or overwhelming psychological trauma. There are, as well, immediate and lasting struggles with belief systems, which start from the moment of encounter with that external threat, and Hiroshima radically alters the balance. For as Edward Glover, a distinguished English psychoanalyst, wrote as early as 1946:

> The first promise of the atomic age is that it can make some of our nightmares come true. The capacity painfully acquired by normal men to distinguish between sleep, delusion, hallucination, and

the objective reality of waking life has for the first time in human history been seriously weakened.[19]

The three elements are also present, although on a different scale, in the Buffalo Creek experience. And the same is even true in regard to schizophrenia. We generally think of schizophrenia as a strictly internal derangement, but it too is subject to external influences, the effort of restitution and the struggle for some kind of meaning structure. Hence the content, style, and impact upon others—the dialogue or non-dialogue between schizophrenic people and society—all this varies enormously with historical time and place. Correspondingly, the end-of-the-world imagery of schizophrenia is strongly affected by historical and technological contest.

III. Schizophrenia as the Key

To explore these psychological issues further, we must return to the question of schizophrenia and its relationship to imagery of the end of the world.

Freud approached the Schreber case from the standpoint of his libido theory. He attributed its paranoid dimension to repressed homosexual wishes—to a strong "wave of libido" directed toward other men. But since this "single proposition: 'I (a man) *love him* (the man)' is completely unacceptable, it is reversed to 'I do not *love* him—I *hate* him'; and that second proposition in turn required, for justification, a third one: 'I do not *love* him—I *hate* him', then via projection, 'He hates me.'" Imagery of world-catastrophe results from the withdrawing of virtually all libido from the external world: "His subjective world has come to an end since his withdrawal of his love from it." Libido or sexual energy was instead directed at the self or more precisely the ego. This reversal of the path of libido Freud called "secondary narcissism." Adult "megalomania" of schizophrenia was due to "a form of 'secondary narcissism' . . . superimposed upon a primary narcissism," which Freud considered a "half-way phase between auto-erotism and object-love," during which the young child directed his libido toward his own body.[20] In schizophrenia one regresses to this infantile stage: the world ends because primary and secondary narcissism prevent love for, or involvement with, anyone or anything in it.

When reading Freud carefully on certain fundamental issues, one finds that his concept assumed more closed or final form in connection with an ongoing ideological struggle. This turns out to be the case with his theory of schizophrenia. At the time he was evolving this theory, Jung was beginning to take issue with his ideas. Jung, his designated "son" and successor, had worked extensively with schizophrenic patients. While Freud's essay on the Schreber case preceded the break between the two men, Freud could not have been unaware of Jung's growing discomfort with Freud's way of applying libido theory to schizophrenia. Eventually Jung was to insist that imagery of the end of the world reflected the psychotic's withdrawal of all interests from the external world, not just his sexuality, and to argue for a more general (more than merely sexual) understanding of the entire concept of libido. Just after his break with Jung, Freud wrote two essays. In one of them, "On Narcissism," Freud stated that applying libido theory to schizophrenia created "a pressing motive for occupying ourselves with the conception of a primary and normal narcissism." He also, somewhat sarcastically, expressed what he took to be Jung's view that "the libido theory has already come to grief in the attempt to explain [schizophrenia]."[21] We may say, then, that Freud's views on imagery of the end of the world were in some measure a defense of—or at least a warding-off of a beginning attack on—his own ideological world.

Similarly, Freud invoked the concept of narcissism in other conditions we might see today as characterized by actual or feared disintegration of the self, by the sense of "falling apart." I have in mind profound forms of depression or "melancholia" and the severe traumatic disorders related to World War I. Freud dealt with both of these syndromes by applying the concept of narcissism, thereby holding to a primacy of libido theory rather than probing death-related issues or what I would call "death equivalents." There were always difficulties with Freud's view of schizophrenia. Even so loyal an explicator of psychoanalytic theory as Otto Fenichel raised questions about the theory of narcissism and reversal of libido, although he did not directly contradict the theory.[22]

Much recent writing questions this classical view and moves in directions closer to my own work. A connecting principle is that of "deanimation"—or what I call desymbolization—the schizophrenic person's sense that his humanity has been taken away from him, that he has been turned into a thing, and that he can experience no actively functioning self. We know that the capacity to experience a vital self has to do with the health of the symbolizing function; one becomes a "thing" when impairment of that function results in extreme concretization and literalization.

Eugen Bleuler, who coined the word *schizophrenia,* gave considerable emphasis to literalizing tendencies, as have most subsequent writers. Burnham, for instance, speaks of the schizophrenic's "references to himself as a toy, puppet, or slave," and of a woman who "spoke of herself as a doll and even moved like a mechanical toy." Another patient told Burnham: "I have lost my soul." And another patient: "It's all a stage production. Everyone is acting and using stage names." And still another: "The people here are only pseudo-people, made of papiermache."[23] Similarly, I was told of a young woman who, describing herself as a machine, would hold out her arms and say, "Smell the plastic and the metal."

While these images may well reflect sensitive perceptions of actual hypocrisy and falsity, they undoubtedly also include long-standing feelings of unreality. They describe a "land of the dead," of a kind many schizophrenics feel themselves to inhabit: the world itself is dead and human history has ended. Again, the death imagery is directly related to desymbolization.

In my own exploration of schizophrenia as well as other psychiatric syndromes, I have stressed three significant areas: death imagery and the simulation of death; the nature of the perceived threat; and the relationship to meaning. R. D. Laing's important early work explores precisely these areas in ways that are not always systematic but nonetheless illuminating.

In *The Divided Self,* Laing provided special insight into schizophrenia as a disorder of feeling—or what I would call a special state of psychic numbing—emphasizing its relationship to psychic death. Put simply, the most extreme inner sense of deadness and unreality equals ultimate psychic numbing equals insanity:

> A man says he is dead but he *is* alive. But his "truth" is that he is dead. . . . When someone says he is an unreal man or that he is

dead, in all seriousness, expressing in radical terms the stark truth of his existence as he experiences it, that is—insanity.[24]

For these patients, "To play possum to feign death, becomes a way of preserving one's aliveness." What Laing calls the "false self" I prefer to call the dead self, or deadened self. That view is in keeping with Laing who, at another point, speaks of "the murder of the self" and of "becoming dead in order not to die."

This "death stance" in schizophrenia differs from the death stance in other psychiatric syndromes, such as depression, where it is also present. Schizophrenia is distinguished by a more profound level of disorder around death imagery, one that has to do with the fear of relationship or vitality. This pervasive imagery leads to a totalization of attitudes, in which relationships themselves become infused with the threat of annihilation. The schizophrenic, then, has a deep ambivalence toward relationships: they are so fraught with terror, even as he seeks them in his desperately lonely state. That is why the schizophrenic one works with is so hard to help.

Concerning the nature of the threat in schizophrenia, Freud, as we have seen, focused on homoerotic impulses and the fear of homosexuality, particularly in paranoid schizophrenia. More recent work, along lines we have begun to discuss, points instead to the threat to existence, to the fear of being annihilated, as central to schizophrenia. This does not mean that sexual confusion and fear of homosexuality are unimportant. But I would argue that they are an aspect of a more general category, rather than themselves the central threat as perceived in schizophrenia.

Macalpine and Hunter, who produced the first full English translation of the Schreber *Memoirs,* also provided a valuable reinterpretation of that case. They took major issue with Freud's view, stressing instead issues around death and life-continuity. They understood Schreber's psychosis as "a reactivation of unconscious, archaic procreation fantasies concerning life, death, immortality, rebirth, creation, including self-impregnation, and accompanied by absolute ambisexuality expressed in doubt and uncertainty about his sex." And they go on to say that "homosexual anxieties were secondary to the primary fantasy of having to be transformed into a woman to be able to procreate." Hence, "Schreber's system centering on creation and the origin of life, whether by God or the sun, sexually or parthenogenetically."

They focused on Schreber's own experience of what he called "soul murder," a theme "of which Freud could make nothing," but one which may well have been "the center of [Schreber's] psychosis." Schreber's own elaboration of "soul murder" makes it clear that he was thinking along lines of death and life-continuity:

> The idea is widespread in the folklore and poetry of all peoples that it is somehow possible to take possession of another person's soul in order to prolong one's life at another soul's expense, or to secure some other advantages which outlast death.[25]

Macalpine and Hunter tell us that, not only was the self being annihilated in soul murder, but so was all possibility of human connection. They saw this as an explanation of Schreber's end-of-the-world fantasy, as well as his delusion that he was immortal ("A person without a soul, i.e. life substance, cannot die"). That fantasy in turn could enable Schreber to imagine himself as "sole survivor to renew mankind." The perception of annihilation remains central.

Similarly, recent work by Harold Searles emphasizes the difficulty schizophrenic persons have in consistently experiencing themselves "as being *alive*." Many do not seem to fear death because "so long as one feels dead anyway . . . one has, subjectively, nothing to lose through death." Yet there can be an accompanying near-total inability to accept the finiteness of life (hence the grandiose delusions of omnipotence and immortality) because of the sense of never having really lived.[26] Behind both experiential deadness and literalized immortality is something close to Schreber's "soul murder," that is, the perpetual dread of annihilation.

The perceived threat of annihilation starts out early in life and may even have a significant genetic component. This perception then becomes totalized, so that for many schizophrenics these early experiences become the whole of life experience. As a result there are profound questions of meaning, desymbolization and deformation which must enter into a theory of schizophrenia. (Much recent American research in the last couple of decades has had to do with family transmission. Some of the work of Wynne, Singer and Lidz emphasizes various forms of transmitted schism or irrationality which I would call desymbolization or deformation.)

The "soul murder" or inner disintegration of schizophrenia gives rise to extreme forms of numbing and deformation throughout the function of the self. At an immediate level, the schizophrenic feels himself flooded with death anxiety that he both embraces and struggles against. At the ultimate level, his absence of connection beyond the self, the sense of being cut off from the Great Chain of Being, from larger human relationships, leaves him with the feeling that life is counterfeit and that biological death is unacceptable and yet uneventful because psychic death is everywhere. Here a form of pseudo-immortality exists as contrasted with what I call a more viable symbolized sense of immortality, of a broader human continuity. This combination of radically impaired meaning and constant threat of annihilation is at the heart of the schizophrenic's imagery of the end of the world. In turn that end-of-the-world imagery is a very central feature in the schizophrenic experience, and by understanding that *process* in schizophrenia, we learn about and can begin to grasp our own end-of-the-world imagery regarding nuclear holocaust. The external threat of contemporary nuclear weapons is approaching the terrain of schizophrenia.

End-of-the-world imagery is something fundamental at the far reaches of the human mind, and I think can be understood as a delicate cutting edge in the balance or imbalance between the struggle against disintegration, on the one hand, and the struggle toward renewal and restitution on the other.

IV. Death and the Continuity of Life: Proximate and Ultimate Levels

To claim, as I have, that schizophrenia has relevance for all end-of-the-world imagery requires the use of a psychological model or paradigm that I would like to outline briefly here. The same paradigm enables us to find common ground among the various end-of-the-world images we have discussed throughout this paper.

The paradigm presumes both a proximate, or immediate, level of experience and an ultimate level close to what Tillich called "ultimate concern." That is, the schizophrenic not only fears annihilation but also, as Searles and others point out, fears (and to some extent welcomes) his being severed from the great stream of

human existence.[27] Indeed this very fear of being historically annihilated is a matter that needs much additional psychological attention.

Our paradigm, then, is that of death and the continuity of
life—or, one may say, the symbolization of life and death. The
proximate level involves the immediate, nitty-gritty experiences
dealt with in most psychological work. The ultimate dimension involves connections beyond the self, reflecting our biological and
historical connectedness, or what I call the symbolization of immortality. In the early Freudian literature, symbolization is a very
primitive defense that one finds in dreams, where one thing represents another. But in the Cassirer–Langer work on symbolization,
it becomes the essence of adult human mentation. Symbolization is
a form of re-creation. Anything we perceive is inwardly re-created
in terms of our entire life experience and our anticipation of the
future. Involved in the struggle for symbolic immortality is the
struggle for connection with those who have gone before and those
who will follow our own limited lifespan.

This sense of immortality is sought normatively through living
on in one's children, one's works, one's human influences and in
something we look on as eternal nature. Continuity is also experienced in religious belief or spiritual principle, whether or not it
literally postulates a life after death; and finally, in any direct experience of transcendence, in psychic states so intense that time
and death disappear. This last case, the classic mode of the
mystics, is not unrelated to various experiences of end-of-the-
world imagery. Such experiential transcendence can be spiritual; it
may be sexual; it can occur through athletics or the contemplation
of beauty. It is sometimes spoken of as "Dionysian," but it can take
quiet forms as well.

Concern with connections beyond the self, what I call the
ultimate dimension, is often left solely to theologians and philosophers. This is a mistake that I feel those of us involved in psychological work should redress. What is involved here is an evolutionary triad. To become human one takes on simultaneously:
first, the knowledge that one dies; second, the symbolizing function which I take to be the fundamental form of human mentation,
requiring the internal re-creation of all that we perceive; and third,
the creation of culture, which is by no means merely a vehicle for
denying death (as many psychoanalytic thinkers, from Freud to

Norman O. Brown have claimed) but is integral to ma
cultural animal, and probably necessary for the developmen
the kind of brain he has come to possess. In struggles around th
symbolization of immortality, then, humankind is struggling with
these three elements, with the levels of psychic experience that
define being human.

The immediate or proximate level of experience involves three
dialectics—those of connection versus separation, movement versus stasis, and integrity versus disintegration. The negative end of
the dialectic is what I call the death equivalent. Each of the three is
familiar, having its beginning or prefiguring in various inchoate experiences from birth and perhaps before. The sequence is from the
physiological (in terms of connection–separation, the newborn
seeking out the breast, and later the mother) to the creation of images (the infant forming pictures of its mother and recognizing
her) to symbolization (the eventual capacity for complex feelings
of love, loyalty—connection). Similarly, the newborn may cry
when physically "separated" from its mother; and the developing
infant, from early images of separation and loss, constructs a
psychological substrate for the slightly later exposure to the idea of
death. Thus over the course of the life cycle, immediate involvements of connection and separation, movement and stasis,
and integrity and disintegration become highly symbolized into
elaborate ethical and psychological constellations.

V. Millennial Imagery and
Contemporary End-of-the-World Dilemmas

We can now ask what people who espouse millennial imagery experience at an ultimate level as well as a proximate one. In what
way does millennial imagery, in its symbolization of immortality,
connect or combine these two levels? How is millennial imagery
related to death equivalents, such as separation, stasis, and
disintegration? What further questions can one raise about the
millennial imagery of clinical syndromes, including schizophrenia?
What is the general relation of millennial imagery to death imagery
and to the experience of inner deadness? How does millennial imagery relate to profound threat, individual or collective? And finally, is there more we can say about millennial imagery in terms of

y? I want to suggest a few general principles
ult questions, rather than attempt anything
em.

d other clinical syndromes, Freud under-
press attempts at what he called "restitution"
to a healthier state. That principle has par-
magery of the end of the world, and in the
Schreber case we saw how that imagery was bound up with the
idea of the world being purified and reconstituted. In millennial
imagery associated with religious thought, the element of
revitalization and moral cleansing—the vision of a new and better
existence—is even more prominent, and considerably more func-
tional. Theological tradition can provide form, coherence, and
shared spiritual experience, in contrast to the isolated delusional
system of the individual schizophrenic person.

Ultimately, we may say that millennial ideas of all kinds are
associated with an even larger category of mythological imagery of
death and rebirth. They represent later theological invocations and
refinements of that earlier, fundamental category. We miss the
significance of millennial imagery if we see in it *only* the threat of
deadness or the absence of meaning; but we also misunderstand it
if we do not recognize in it precisely that threat and absence. In
other words, millennial imagery always includes something on the
order of death equivalents—of threatened annihilation—and at
the same time, in its various symbolizations, something on the
order of renewal and revitalization.

In schizophrenia that imagery of revitalization is radically
literalized. The issue of literalization, as an aspect of overall
desymbolization, has general significance for schizophrenia. With
desymbolization there is an inability to carry out the specific
human task of constant creation and re-creation of images and
forms, or what I call the formative-symbolizing function. What is
called the "thought disorder" of schizophrenia involves a fundamental impairment to this function, the replacement of symbolic
flow with static literalization.

An important question for religious millennial imagery is the extent to which it is experienced in literalized, as opposed to more
formative or symbolized, ways. I had a conversation about this
question with Paul Tillich toward the end of his life. We talked
particularly about Christian imagery of immortality. Tillich's view

was that the more literal promise of an "after-life" was a c
form of theological expression, disseminated among the relati
poor and uneducated. In the more profound expressions of thi
imagery, Tillich held, the idea of immortality symbolized unending
spiritual continuity. Many, to be sure, would argue with this view,
and it is undoubtedly more true at certain moments of history than
others. But it does help us to grasp distinctions among different expressions of millennial thought, as well as connecting principles.
And when a millennial vision becomes so literalized that it is
associated with a prediction of the actual end of the world on a
particular day on the basis of biblical images or mathematical
calculation applied to such images, we become aware of a dis-
quieting border area of theology and psychopathology.[28]

The appearance of nuclear weapons in the mid-1940s evoked an
image: that of man's extermination of himself as a species with his
own technology. The image, of course, is not totally new. Versions
of it have been constituted by visionaries—H. G. Wells is an
outstanding example—at least from the time of the Industrial
Revolution or before. But nuclear weapons gave substance to the
image and disseminated it everywhere, making it the dubious
psychic property of the average human being.

Moreover, the element of self-extermination must be differentiated from older religious images of Armageddon, "Final Judgment," or the "end of the world." Terrifying as these may be, they
are part of a worldview or cosmology—man is acted upon by a
higher power who has his reasons, who destroys only for spiritual
purposes (such as achieving "the kingdom of God"). That is a far
cry from man's destruction of himself with his own tools, and to
no purpose.

There are several special features to this contemporary end-of-
the-world imagery. There is first the suggestion of the end of our
species, of something on the order of biological extinction. Second, it is related to specific external events of recent history
(Hiroshima and Nagasaki as well as the Nazi death camps). And
third, unlike earlier imagery of world-destruction—even that
associated with such external events as the medieval plagues—the
danger comes from our own hand, from man and his technology.
The source is not God or nature, but we ourselves. Our "end" is in

erceived as a form of self-destruction. We
little justification or significance. If some
as inevitable, they do so with resignation
posed to the meaningful inevitability of an
mission to the awesome forces of nature.
destruction has bearing on issues of wide-
ll as psychic numbing. The numbing
—diminished feeling with denial—takes place not only in relationship to massive death, but also around the idea of human responsibility for that process. The source is not God or Nature, but we
ourselves. Perhaps we don't know how to gauge, as yet, what this
recognition or this half-recognition is doing to us. There is now
considerable research being done, but we must begin to raise questions about numbing, or diminished capacity for feeling, and
about guilt. Today we are put in the position of imagining
ourselves being both executioner and victim, the two roles Camus
warned us never to assume, for there is numbing both toward the
destruction itself and our guilt as potential perpetrators of that
destruction. Traditionally, guilt is relatively contained within an
eschatology: if man is guilty, he must be punished, he must be
destroyed in order to be re-created in purer form. Within our present context, however, one perceives a threat of a literal, absolute
end without benefit of a belief system that gives form, acceptance,
or solace to that idea.

This predicament takes us back to some of the questions mentioned earlier. Anticipating the possibility of nuclear holocaust, we
experience profound doubts about our larger human connectedness (the ultimate dimension in our paradigm). For in a
post-nuclear world, one can hardly be certain of living on in one's
children or their children; in one's creations or human influences;
in some form of lasting spirituality (which may not be possible in
connection with an imagined world in which there are virtually
none among the biologically living); or in eternal nature, which we
know to be susceptible to our weapons and pollutions.

The radical uncertainty of these four modes may indeed play a
large part in our present hunger for direct experiences of transcendence—whether through drugs, meditation, or other altered
states of consciousness. Similarly, there is a growing body of
evidence relating perceptions of nuclear threat to different versions
of what I have called death equivalents—imagery of separation,

stasis, and disintegration. All of these, of course, become bound up with different forms of psychic numbing, or with something worse: with a pseudo-religion I call "nuclearism" involving the deification and worship of the very agents of our potential destruction, seeing in them a deity that can not only destroy but also protect and create, even depending on them to keep us and the world going.[29] Evidence of this exists in written accounts about nuclear weapons, the beautiful descriptions of the mushroom cloud, its elegance and protective function as it shields us from all future wars. Or consider the attitudes and stances taken toward nuclear weapons by scenario writers in terms of *never* rejecting the use of one of them in some form. It is the ultimate paradox in human existence—the worship of the agent of our potential annihilation.

The extent of nuclearism is difficult to gauge, but it diffuses itself all through our culture. What I call the "retirement syndrome" is one example of the pervasiveness of nuclearism. Recently in 1982, when forced to retire at the age of eighty-one, Admiral Hyman B. Rickover, generally characterized as "the father of America's nuclear navy," stated that nuclear weapons should be outlawed. He further stated that "I think we'll probably destroy ourselves" and that "I'm not proud of the part I played." One has to assume psychologically that the man–weapons constellation is so pervasive while a person is in office, the pattern of nuclearism so dominant, that the world is seen through a prism of nuclear weapons and therefore nuclear weapons-centered policies are promulgated. At the moment of retirement, however, a person can take a step back, look at the matter with sufficient detachment, question assumptions, and voice doubts previously suppressed.

Of course Rickover was not the first. Eisenhower's famous warning about the military-industrial complex was a retirement speech. Others include Oppenheimer who initially favored using the bomb—and blocked early scientific opposition to its use without warning on a populated city—but later considered the new H-bomb weapons system the primary responsibility of someone else, and of course Henry Stimson. Secretary of War at the time the bomb was first used, Stimson referred privately to the weapons as the "dreadful," the "awful," and the "diabolical." He even arranged to have available to him a subordinate whose task was mainly to listen to his pained concerns about the weapons. Yet, he never wavered in his determination that the bomb be used, and he arranged committee deliberations such that it was a foregone conclusion. Among his last acts before leaving office, however, was a memorandum about the bomb in which he described it as "merely a first step in a control by man over the forces of nature too revolutionary and dangerous to fit into the old concept," and he urged that we "enter into an arrangement with the Russians, the general purpose of which would be to control and limit the use of the atomic bomb as an instrument of war. . . ."[30]

These examples indicate not only the pervasiveness of nuclearism but also the possibility of transformation away from it. It is not surprising that the weapons would become objects of worship, because they can do what only God could do before, i.e., destroy the world. They are also our ultimate technology, and blind worship of technology has become for many a source of salvation and resolution for all our conflicts, those very conflicts from which we could draw end-of-the-world imagery.

Yet our exploration of end-of-the-world imagery suggests, in itself, a countering force. It is a precarious one, to be sure, because it hovers on the anxious edge of ultimate destruction. Consider the two dimensions of the Dr. Strangelove image. There is on the one hand the impulse to "press the button" and "get the thing over with," even the orgiastic excitement of the wild forces let loose —destroying everything in order to feel alive. But the other side of the Strangelove image, what I take to be its wisdom, is the insistence that we confront the radical absurdity or "madness" of the world-destruction we are contemplating. It is similar to what Teilhard de Chardin, as an evolutionary theorist and mystic, had in mind in writing about the expansion of the "noosphere" or area of knowledge as the other side of our capacity to destroy ourselves. And it is what Erik Erikson means when he speaks about the relationship between our destructive capacity and our first glimpses of a form of human identity so inclusive that it embraces the entire species.[31]

We must imagine something close to nuclear extinction in order to prevent it. We must extend our psychological and moral imaginations in order to hold off precisely what we begin to imagine.

Eugene Rabinowitz provides us with a very good example of just this possibility for renewal, when he writes about the circumstances in which he and other nuclear scientists drafted one of the earliest petitions against the use of a nuclear weapon:

> In the summer of 1945, some of us walked the streets of Chicago vividly imagining the sky suddenly lit up by a giant fireball, the steel skeleton of sky scrapers bending into grotesque shapes and their masonry raining into the streets below, until a great cloud of dust rose and settled onto the crumbling city.[32]

This image of the "end of the world" inspired him to urge his colleagues to return quickly to their work on the "Franck Report" that he, Franck, Szilard and a number of others in Chicago were instrumental in creating. To be sure, the Report's recommendation that the atomic weapon not be used on a human population without warning was not heeded. But it has become a central document in our contemporary struggle to imagine the end of the world in order to preserve it.

1.   Robert Jay Lifton, *Death in Life: Survivors of Hiroshima* (New York: Touchstone, 1976 [1968]), p. 21.

2.   Ibid., p. 22.

3.   Ibid.

4.   Y. Ota, *Shikabane no machi* (Town of Corpses) (Tokyo: Kawadi Shobō, 1955), p. 63.

5.   Lifton, *Death in Life,* p. 23.

6.   Ibid.

7.   See original manuscript of *Hiroshima Diary,* p. 4.

8.   Ota, *Shikabane no machi,* p. 63.

9.   Hachiya, *Hiroshima Diary,* pp. 4, 5, 37.

10.   Lifton, *Death in Life,* p. 27.

11.   Ibid., p. 29.

12.   See Robert Jay Lifton and Eric Olson, "The Human Meaning of Total Disaster: The Buffalo Creek Experience," *Psychiatry* 39 (February 1976): 1–18. See also Kai T. Erikson, *Everything in its Path* (New York: Simon & Schuster, 1979); and James L. Titchener and Frederic T. Kapp, "Family and Character Change in Buffalo Creek," *American Journal of Psychiatry* 133/4 (March 1976): 295–99.

13.   Lifton and Olson, "The Human Meaning of Total Disaster," p. 13.

14.   Ibid.

15.   Daniel Paul Schreber, *Memoirs of My Nervous Illness,* ed. and trans. Ida Macalpine and Richard A. Hunter (London: Wm. Dawson & Sons, Ltd., 1955 [1903]), pp. 84–85.

16.   Ibid., pp. 85–88.

17.   Ibid.

18. Lifton, *Death in Life,* pp. 479–539, 367–95, 525–39.

19. Edward Glover, *War, Sadism, and Pacifism* (London: George Allen & Unwin, 1946), p. 274.

20. Sigmund Freud, "Psycho-analytic Notes on an Autobiographical Account of a Case of Paranoia (Dimentia Paranoides)" [1911], in *The Standard Edition of the Complete Psychological Works of Sigmund Freud,* ed. James Strachey, 24 vols. (London: The Hogarth Press and the Institute of Psycho-analysis, 1953–1974), 12 : 70.

21. Freud, "On Narcissism: An Introduction," in *The Standard Edition,* 14 : 74. See also Sheldon T. Selesnick, "C. G. Jung's Contributions to Psychoanalysis," *American Journal of Psychiatry* 120 (1963): 350–56.

22. Otto Fenichel, *The Psychoanalytic Theory of Neurosis* (New York: W. W. Norton, 1945), pp. 417–18, 424–25.

23. Donald O. Burnham, "Separation Anxiety," *Archives of General Psychiatry* 13 (1965): 346–58.

24. R. D. Laing, *The Divided Self* (Baltimore: Penguin [Pelican], 1965).

25. Schreber, *Memoirs,* p. 55.

26. Harold F. Searles, *Collected Papers on Schizophrenia and Related Subjects* (New York: International Universities Press, 1965), pp. 488–89, 497.

27. There can be an element of ecstasy in the schizophrenic perception of the end of the world, along with its terror. The same has been found to be true for other aspects of schizophrenic experience.

28. Today in this country, there are cults that claim biblical imagery and attach it to nuclear danger, welcoming nuclear holocaust as a way of cleansing ourselves of our sins. These cults maintain the fantasy that they, the true believers, will somehow survive. This of course is literalization, and it is a loss or a renunciation of the regenerative dimensions of millennial imagery.

29. In my book *The Broken Connection* (New York: Simon & Schuster, 1979), I elaborate in much greater detail these and other issues discussed throughout this paper. See especially Chapters 1, 2, 16, 22 and 23, and Appendices A, C, and D.

30. Gar Alperovitz, *Atomic Diplomacy: Hiroshima and Potsdam* (New York: Simon & Schuster, 1965), pp. 276–79.

31. Erik Erikson, "A Developmental Crisis of Mankind," unpublished manuscript.

32. Eugene Rabinowitz, "Five Years After," in *The Atomic Age,* ed. Mortin Grodzins and Eugene Rabinowitz (New York: Basic Books, 1963), p. 156.

DENISE LEVERTOV

The voice of political conscience is staple in work of British-born poet Denise Levertov. Born in 1923 and privately educated, Levertov is one of the best-known and most respected living poets. Her career includes public readings, teaching at Brandeis and Stanford Universities, and translating works by contemporary Spanish and French poets.

Granted American citizenship in 1956, she became active in the anti-war movement of the 60s. While her husband Mitchell Goodman went to trial with Benjamin Spock for anti-war protests, Levertov took off on peace missions to Bulgaria and North Vietnam.

Now in her early sixties, Levertov has turned librettist. With Boston composer Newell Hendricks, she is author of the oratorio "El Salvador," based on the murder of Archbishop Romero and four Roman Catholic churchwomen.

Passionate and poetic, Levertov is descended from a Welsh mystic—Angel Jones of Mold—and from the noted Hasid Schneur Zalman, the Rav of Northern White Russia. These mystical/intellectual forebears, says Levertov, "have given me a sense of marvel. In both traditions there was joy in the physical world, a sense of wonder at creation. That's what my poems are about."

Poetry Reading

To Speak

To speak of sorrow
works upon it
                    moves it from its
crouched place barring
the way to and from the soul's hall—

out in the light it
shows clear, whether
shrunken or known as
a giant wrath—
                    discrete
at least, where before

its great shadow joined
the walls and roof and seemed
to uphold the hall like a beam.

The Novices

They enter the bare wood, drawn
by a clear-obscure summons they fear
and have no choice but to heed.

A rustling underfoot, a
long trail to go, the thornbushes grow
across the dwindling paths.

Until the small clearing, where they
anticipate violence, knowing some rite
to be performed, and compelled to it.

The man moves forward, the boy
sees what he means to do: from an oaktree
a chain runs at an angle into earth

and they pit themselves to uproot it,
dogged and frightened, to pull the iron
out of the earth's heart.

But from the further depths of the wood
as they strain and weigh on the great chain
appears the spirit,

the wood-demon who summoned them.
And he is not bestial, not fierce
but an old woodsman,

gnarled, shabby, smelling of smoke and sweat,
of a bear's height and shambling like a bear.
Yet his presence is a spirit's presence

and awe takes their breath.
Gentle and rough, laughing a little,
he makes his will known:

not for an act of force he called them,
for no rite of obscure violence
but that they might look about them

and see intricate branch and bark,
stars of moss and the old scars
left by dead men's saws,

and not ask what that chain was.
To leave the open fields
and enter the forest,

that was the rite.
Knowing there was mystery, they could go.
Go back now! And he receded

among the multitude of forms,
the twists and shadows they saw now, listening
to the hum of the world's wood.

Who Is at My Window

> Who is at my window, who, who?
> Go from my window, go, go!
> Who calleth there so like a stranger?
> Go from my window, go!
> J. WEDDERBURN
> 1542

Who is at my window, who, who?
It's the blind cuckoo, mulling
  he old song over.

The old song is about fear, about
tomorrow and next year.

Timor mortis conturbat me, he sings
What's the use?   He brings me

the image of **when**, a boat
hull down, smudged on the darkening ocean.

I want to move deeper into today;
he keeps me from that work.
Today and eternity are nothing to him.
His wings spread at the window make it dark.

Go from my window, go, go!

Three Meditations

i

the only object is
a man, carved
out of himself, so wrought he
fills his given space, makes
traceries sufficient to
others' needs
            (here is
social action, for the poet,
anyway, his
politics, his
news)
CHARLES OLSON

Breathe deep of the
freshly gray morning air, mild
spring of the day.
Let the night's dream-planting
bear leaves
and light up the death-mirrors with
shining petals.
Stand fast in thy place:
remember, Caedmon
turning from song was met
in his cow-barn by One who set him
to sing the beginning.

Live
in thy fingertips and in thy
hair's rising; hunger
be thine, food
be thine and what wine
will not shrivel thee.
Breathe deep of
evening, be with the
rivers of tumult, sharpen
thy wits to know power and be
humble.

ii

The task of the poet is to make clear
to *himself,* and thereby to others,
the temporal and eternal questions.
IBSEN

Barbarians
throng the straight roads of
my empire, converging
on black Rome.
There is darkness in me.
Silver sunrays
sternly, in tenuous joy
cut through its folds:
mountains
arise from cloud.
Who was it yelled, cracking
the glass of delight?
Who sent the child
sobbing to bed, and woke it
later to comfort it?
I, I, I, I.
I multitude, I tyrant,
I angel, I you, you
world, battlefield, stirring
with unheard litanies, sounds of piercing

green half-smothered by
strewn bones.

iii

And virtue? Virtue lies in the heroic
response to the creative wonder, the
utmost response.
D. H. LAWRENCE

Death in the grassblade
a dull
substance, heading blindly
for the bone

and bread preserved without
virtue,
sweet grapes sour to the children's children.

We breathe an ill wind,
nevertheless our kind
in mushroom multitudes
jostles for elbow-room
moonwards

an equalization of
hazards
bringing the poet
back to song
as before

to sing of death
as before
and life, while he
has it, energy

being in him a singing,
a beating of gongs, efficacious
to drive away devils,
response to

the wonder that
as before
shows a double face,

to be
what he is
being his virtue

filling his whole space
so no devil
may enter.

On the 32nd Anniversary
of the Bombing of Hiroshima and Nagasaki

A new bomb, big one, drops
a long way beyond the fence of our minds'
property. And they tell us, '*With this
the war is over.*'
                    We are twenty years old, thereabouts—
now stale uniforms
can fall off our backs, replaced
by silk of youth! Relief,
not awe, gasps from our
mouths and widens
ignorant eyes. We've been used
to the daily recitation of death's
multiplication tables: we don't notice
the quantum leap: eighty-seven thousand
killed outright by a single bomb,
fifty-one thousand missing or injured.
We were nurses, refugees, sailors, soldiers,
familiar with many guises of death: war had ended our
                                                childhood.
We knew about craters, torpedoes, gas ovens.
This we ignored.
The rumor was distant traffic. Louder

were our heartbeats,
                    summer was springtime:
'The war is over!'

And on the third day no-one
rose from the dead at Hiroshima,
and at Nagasaki
the exploit was repeated, as if
to insist we take notice:
seventy-three thousand
killed by one bomb,
seventy-four thousand injured or missing.

Familiar simple-arithmetic of
mortal flesh did not serve,
                    yet I cannot remember,
and Sid, Ruth, Betty, Matthew, Virginia
cannot remember August sixth or
August ninth, nineteen-
forty-five. *The war was over* was all we knew
and a vague wonder, *what next? What will ordinary
life be like, now ordinary life as we know it
is gone?*

But the shadow,
the human shadowgraph sinking itself
indelibly upon stone at Hiroshima
as a man, woman or child was consumed
in unearthly fire—
                    that shadow
already had been for three days
imprinted upon our lives.
Three decades now we have lived
with its fingers outstretched in horror clinging
to our future, our children's future,
into history or the void.
The shadow's voice
cries out to us to cry out.
Its nails dig
                    into our souls

to wake them:
'*Something,*' it ceaselessly
repeats, its silence
a whisper, its whisper
a shriek,
      while 'the radiant gist'
is lost, and the moral labyrinths of
humankind convulse as if made
of snakes clustered and intertwined and stirring
from long sleep—
'... *something can yet*

be salvaged upon the earth:
try, try to survive,
try to redeem
the human vision
from cesspits where human hands
have thrown it, as I was thrown
from life into shadow. . . .'

The Sun Going Down upon Our Wrath

You who are so beautiful—
your deep and childish faces,
your tall bodies—

Shall I warn you?

Do you know
what it was to have
a certitude of grasses waving
upon the earth though all
humankind were dust?
Of dust returning
to fruitful dust?

Do you already know

what hope is fading from us
and pay no heed,
see the detested grave-worm shrivel,
the once-despised,
and not need it?

Is there an odyssey
your feet pull you towards
away from now to walk
the waters, the fallen
orchard stars?
                    It seems
your fears are only the old fears, antique
anxieties, how graceful;
they lay as cloaks on shoulders
of men long dead,
skirts of sorrow wrapped
over the thighs of legendary women.

Can you be warned?

If you are warned will your beauty
scale off, to leave
gaping meat livid with revulsion?

No, who can believe it.
Even I in whose heart
stones rattle, rise each day
to work and imagine.

Get wisdom, get understanding, saith
the ancient. But he believed
there is nothing new under the sun,
his future
rolled away in great coils forever
into the generations.
Among conies the grass
grew again
and among bones.
And the bones would rise.

If there is time to warn you,
if you believed there shall be
never again a green blade in the crevice,
luminous eyes in rockshadow:
if you were warned and believed
the warning,

would your beauty
break into spears of fire,

fire to turn fire, a wall
of refusal, could there be
a reversal I cannot

hoist myself high enough
to see,
plunge myself deep enough
to know?

Forest Altar, September

The gleam of thy drenched
floors of leaf-layers! Fragrance
of death and change!
            If there is only
now to live, I'll live
the hour till doomstroke
crouched with the russet toad,
my huge human size
no more account than a bough fallen:

not upward,
searching for branch-hidden sky:
I'll look
down into paradise.

Thy moss gardens, the deep

constellations of green, the striate
rock furred with emerald,
inscribed with gold lichen,
with scarlet!
             Thy smooth
acorns in roughsurfaced
precise cups!
             Thy black
horns of plenty!

The Great Wave

With my brother I ran
willingly into the sea:

our mother, our sister too,
all of us free and naked.

We knew nothing of risk,
only the sacred pleasure

of sun and sand and the
beckoning ocean:

in, into the leaping
green of the lilt of it.

But at once a vast wave
unfurled itself to seize me, furled

about me, bore me as a bubble
back and tilted aslant from

all shore; all sight, sound, thought of others swept
instantly into

remote distance—

Now is wholly
this lucent rampart up which

I can't climb but where
I cling, powerless, unable

to distinguish terror from delight, calm
only in the one wanhope, to keep

a breath alive above the enormous
roar of the sunlaughing utter

force of the great wave, ride
on in its dangerous cradle of swift
transparent silks that curve
in steel over and round me, bearing

westward, outward, beyond
all shores, the great

wave still mounting, moving,
poised and poised in its

flood of emerald, dark unshatterable
crystal of its

unfathomed purpose—

Re-Rooting

We were trying to put the roots back,
wild and erratic straying root-limbs,
trying to fit them into the hole that was
cleancut in clay, deep but not
wide enough; or wide but too square—trying
to get the roots back into earth

before they dried out and died.
Ineptly we pulled and pushed
striving to encompass so many rivers
of wood and fiber in one confinement without
snapping the arteries of sap, the force
of life springing in them that made them
spring away from our hands—
we knew our own life was
tied to that strength, that strength we knew would
ebb away if we could not find within us
the blessed guile to tempt
its energy back into earth,
into the quiet depths from which we had
rashly torn it, and now clumsily
struggled to thrust it back not into sinuous corridors
fit for its subtleties, but obstinately
into an excavation dug by machine.
                    And I wake,
as if from dream, but discover
even this digging, better than nothing,
has not yet begun.

Writing in the Dark

It's not difficult.
Anyway, it's necessary.

Wait till morning, and you'll forget.
And who knows if morning will come.

Fumble for the light, and you'll be
stark awake, but the vision
will be fading, slipping
out of reach.

You must have paper at hand,

a felt-tip pen—ballpoints don't always flow,
pencil points tend to break. There's nothing
shameful in that much prudence: those are your tools.

Never mind about crossing your t's, dotting your i's—
but take care not to cover
one word with the next. Practice will reveal
how one hand instinctively comes to the aid of the other
to keep each line
clear of the next.

Keep writing in the dark:
a record of the night, or
words that pulled you from depths of unknowing,
words that flew through your mind, strange birds
crying their urgency with human voices,

or opened
as flowers of a tree that blooms
only once in a lifetime:

words that may have the power
to make the sun rise again.

Age of Terror

Between the fear
of the horror of Afterwards
and the despair
in the thought of no Afterwards,
we move abraded,
each gesture scraping us
on the millstones.

In dream
there was an Afterwards:
    the unknown device—

a silver computer as big as a
block of offices at least,
                              floating
like Magritte's castle on its rock, aloft
in blue sky—
   did explode,
                    there was
a long moment of cataclysm,
                                light
of a subdued rose-red suffused
all the air before
a rumbling confused darkness ensued,
but
I came to,
         face down,
                    and found
my young sister alive near me,
and knew my still younger brother
and our mother and father
                         were close by too,
and, passionately relieved, I
comforted my shocked sister,
                         still not daring
to raise my head,

only stroking and kissing her arm,
afraid to find devastation around us
though we, all five of us,
seemed to have survived—and I readied myself
to take rollcall: 'Paul Levertoff? Beatrice Levertoff?'

And then in dream—not knowing
if this device, this explosion, were radioactive or not,
but sure that where it had centered
there must be wreck, terror,
fire and dust—
the millstones
commenced their grinding again,

and as in daylight

again we were held between them, cramped,
scraped raw by questions:

perhaps, indeed, we were safe; perhaps
no worse was to follow?—but ...
what of our gladness, when there,
    where the core of the strange
    roselight had flared up
    out of the detonation of brilliant
    angular silver,
there must be others, others in agony,
and as in waking daylight,
the broken dead?

About Political Action in Which
Each Individual Acts from the Heart

When solitaries draw close, releasing
each solitude into its blossoming,

when we give to each other the roses
of our communion—

a culture of gardens, horticulture not agribusiness,
arbors among the lettuce, small terrains—

when we taste in small victories sometimes
the small, ephemeral yet joyful
harvest of our striving,

great power flows from us,
luminous, a promise. Yes! ... Then

great energy flows from solitude,
and great power from communion.

What It Could Be

Uranium, with which we know
only how to destroy,

lies always under
the most sacred lands—

Australia, Africa, America,
wherever it's found is found an oppressed
ancient people who knew
long before white men found and named it
that there under their feet

under rock, under mountain, deeper
than deepest watersprings, under
the vast deserts familiar
inch by inch to their children

lay a great power.
                     And they knew the folly
of wresting, wrestling, ravaging from the earth
that which it kept
               so guarded.

Now, now, now at this instant,
men are gouging lumps of that power, that presence,
out of the tortured planet the ancients
say is our mother.
                   Breaking the doors
of her sanctum, tearing the secret
out of her flesh.

But left to lie, its metaphysical weight
might in a million years have proved
benign, its true force being to be
a clue to righteousness—

showing forth
the human power
not to kill, to choose
not to kill: to transcend
the dull force of our weight and will;

that known profound presence, *un*touched,
the sign
providing witness,
      occasion,
        ritual
for the continuing act of
*non*violence, of passionate
reverence, active love.

An English Field in the Nuclear Age

To render it!—*this* moment,
                haze and halos of
        sunbless'd particulars, knowing
no one,
    not lost and dearest nor
    the unfound,
could,
    though summoned,
    though present,
partake nor proffer vision unless
           (named, spun, tempered, stain of it
            sunk into steel of utterance) it
      be wrought:
(centuries furrowed in oakbole, *this* oak,
these dogrose pallors, that very company
      of rooks plodding
        from stile to stile of the sky):
to render that isolate knowledge, certain
    (shadow of oakleaves, larks
    urging the green wheat into spires)

there is no sharing save in the furnace,
the transubstantiate, acts
                          of passion:
                                    (the way
          air, *this* minute, searches
          warm bare shoulders, blind, a lover,

          and how among
          thistles, nettles, subtle silver
          of long-dried cowpads,

          gold mirrors of buttercup satin
          assert eternity as they reflect

          nothing, everything, absolute instant,
          and dread

          holds its breath, for
          this minute at least was
          not the last).

Candles in Babylon

Through the midnight streets of Babylon
between the steel towers of their arsenals,
between the torture castles with no windows,
we race by barefoot, holding tight
our candles, trying to shield
the shivering flames, crying
'Sleepers Awake!'
                    hoping
the rhyme's promise was true,
that we may return
from this place of terror
home to a calm dawn and
the work we had just begun.

MARY WATKINS

Mary Watkins, Ph.D., is a clinical and developmental psychologist practicing in Littleton and Cambridge, Massachusetts. Born in 1950 in Texas, Dr. Watkins is a Research Associate in the Department of Psychology, Clark University. Her publications include a widely acclaimed study of the power of images called *Waking Dreams* and, most recently, *Invisible Guests: The Development of Imaginal Dialogues.*

"In Dreams Begin Responsibilities"
Moral Imagination and Peace Action

Delmore Schwartz, with all his Yeatsian influence, entitled a volume of short stories *In Dreams Begin Responsibilities,* and a cycle of poems "The Dreams Which Begin in Responsibilities." Dreams begin responsibilities, responsibilities dreams. What are some of the meanings of these phrases as we face the threat of nuclear apocalypse? What are the relations between image and responsibility, imagination and peace and disarmament action?

I.

Let us begin with "in dreams begin responsibilities." With respect to the possibility of nuclear war, many psychologically-minded writers—Fromm, Lifton, Mack, Macy, Boulding, and others—have stressed the importance of imagination in preventing nuclear war, seeing quietism in relation to the possibility of nuclear war as a failure or inadequacy of so-called "moral imagination." How is this so? First of all, it is only through imagination that the dimensions of the Third and last World War could *possibly* be approached, as nothing that has ever taken place—not even the horrific annihilations at Hiroshima, Nagasaki, and Dresden—can anticipate it fully. So vast. So perhaps even *un*imaginable it would be. Secondly, as the Romantics pointed out, the imagination approaches facts in a different manner than reason does. Whereas the latter focuses on the general and the abstract, the imagination brings to life the particular—particular scenes with particular characters. In so doing, it moves the heart. The imagination's way into perceiving nuclear war is not the rhetoric of numbers, technological jargon and probabilities (which numb one), but it is of specific images, particular losses.

It is also only through imagination that we can entertain the possibility that these weapons could be dismantled in the name of peace, as never before have weapons been made and not used. It requires a utopic imagination, an imagination which does not simply mirror the world but which can create what the Romantics called a heterocosm—a world other than this one—which, once alive imaginally, can inspire action.[1]

Imagination has also been seen as critical in breaking down the divisions between one nation and another, in particular between American citizens and those of the Soviet Union. For through imagination we can escape our bodily limitations and identify with others—the others who, as Lifton points out, would be the likely objects of our weapons. Through sympathetic identification we can begin to break the process of dehumanizing the other that occurs when he is seen only from the external point of view.

Critical to the role of imagination in inhibiting nuclear war is its spontaneously compensatory aspect, pointed out by nineteenth-century psychologists. Imagination brings to our awareness the forgotten, the extruded, that which is undervalued by consciousness or defended against. As Michael Carey's work documents, in spite of our attempts to disregard or minimize the nuclear danger, disturbing, nightmarish imagery does break through in our dreams and thoughts, turning attention—even if only momentarily—to our desperate situation.[2] In dreams I have collected on nuclear war, the Jewish holocaust is often linked to the nuclear holocaust, dissolving the distinction between Jews and non-Jews. We are all Jews beneath the falling bomb. There is no special dispensation. Dreams place us amidst the rubble of something we have loved—a medieval city, the Metropolitan Museum, a street of our home town. There are dreams where we cannot move or talk, dying slowly as we are of internal contamination, radiation sickness—alone, without comfort. These unbidden images need only the sound of an approaching airplane or a moment of nausea to take root, to unfold.

Imagination's anticipatory, utopic, sympathetic, and compensatory nature extends us into the very nuclear world we try to escape from, defend against. In doing so, this nature awakens an Enlightenment and Romantic idea of the imagination as moral.

Philosophers and poets claimed this morality for imagination because it was held to be the residence of "sympathy," that is, the capacity to place oneself into other situations and beings in order to experience their reality and feelings. Shelley argued for the moral importance of poetry, and imagination in general. In his *Defense of Poetry* he proposed that

> A man to be greatly good must imagine intensely and comprehensively; he must put himself in the place of another and of many others; the pains and pleasures of his species must become his own. The great instrument of moral good is the imagination. . . . [3]

But there was a strange transformation in this concept of moral imagination. Earlier writers in this period (like Adam Smith) saw such sympathetic participation as the root of moral action. Later Shelley thought that it was not the image that inspired moral action to benefit the other, but that it was the very act of imagining which affects the other. Then poets like Keats were involved in such sympathetic identifications, not for another's sake, but purely for their own interest in the chameleon-like mind. Keats describes looking out the window from his writing desk and becoming the sparrow he sees, pecking at the gravel. Keats contended that the true poet has no character or identity of his own, annihilated as he is in the characters around him. [4] These Romantic poets held Shakespeare as their ideal, extolling his Proteus-like ability, claiming that it was this quality of imagination that makes the poet transcendent. The Romantic Henry Hazlitt said of Shakespeare: "He had only to think of anything in order to become that thing with all the circumstances belonging to it." [5] Hazlitt, Novalis, Coleridge, Blake, Shelling and others saw the imagination as freeing us from a self-centered world. [6]

This notion of moral and sympathetic imagination ran amuck by the end of the Romantic period due to the goal all too often imposed on such imagining: to expand the limits of the self by this chameleon-like activity, to enrich the self with the bounty of the world. That which was originally linked to action—sympathetic imagination—became alienated from it. This alienation of imagination from moral action, due to the Romantics' focus on self-realization, has profoundly influenced our twentieth-century view of imagination.

In psychoanalysis we no longer find the imagination lauded for its ability to transport us into the world's concerns and others' sufferings, but rather for the reverse. Imagination is seen as a preserve of wishes, the self's wishes which stand in stark contrast to the realities outside and, indeed, which defend us against the harshness of the external world. Work with images within psychology has been exclusively focused on improving the self—psychologically, spiritually, physically. It is little wonder that Soviet psychology berates our psychology of imagination as "bourgeois."[7]

Our twentieth-century psychology has demoralized the imagination through its individualistic focus, its subjectivistic reduction of images which reflect the crisis of the world back into the personal history and intrapsychic dynamics of the patient; and often its naïve faith in the "evolution of consciousness" which contradicts facts and experience. If we look at the recent history of the uses of imagination, we find ourselves in the Romantics' dilemma again —imagination is seen as panacea. We are directed to entertain images to cure cancer, sexual impotence, warts, stress, insecurity, lack of productivity—images to increase personal power, solve personal history, enhance personal growth. In this tradition, entertaining nuclear images could become just one more exercise in the growth arena. Images which in their singleness could help move one to action now in their proliferation defend us from it, keep us occupied with our interior journeying, journal writing and dream interpretation.

If we take the claim that imagination is intrinsically moral, we can poignantly see the problem with Romantic hyperbole. For is not imagination as responsible for the building of Auschwitz as it is for the founding of the United Nations; isn't it as active in an actual rape as it is in a moment of sympathetic compassion? Ironically, the sympathetic imagination was credited by some in the nineteenth century for beginning to unite the classes in Germany. But it was just such a solidarity that made it possible for Germany to take on the rest of the world in our own century—to engage in an "us versus them" mentality which was pathologically devoid of sympathetic identification.

So it is interesting that, in the midst of a century that has turned imagination into an egocentrically oriented faculty, we begin to hear again of a "moral imagination." Perhaps with this in mind, we can propose a different notion of moral imagination. Not all imaginings are moral in and of themselves. Some serve to sustain our narcissism and self-centeredness, as psychoanalysis amply shows. Some imaginings, by virtue of their structure, do prompt the moral sense, precisely by their quality of "sympathy," of letting us feel realities apart from the self's. Others prompt the moral sense through their anticipatory, compensatory, or utopic functions.

But for the imagining to be moral, I believe, it must have another component, and that is action. It is not enough for our heart to be stirred by an image—shall we say of a little Hiroshima girl, burnt, orphaned, surrounded by the carnage of everything she's known. That heart-stirring has an implicit movement toward action in it that must be nurtured. Otherwise, as Donald Moss has pointed out, we use these images perversely: "to get off" on the "erotics of destruction."[8] Or we use them to "develop the self" ("Well, now I'm in touch with the nuclear thing. I think I'll take a weekend workshop next month on. . .").

Yet, we can't just append action to any image and come up with moral imagination—images do not necessarily have intrinsic moral value. How we respond to them, act or refrain from action with regard to them, is crucial. Responsibilities can begin in a person's dreams and images, but they cannot be fulfilled there. As the Romantic experience teaches us, we can use imagination's capacity for sympathy either as a stimulus for moral action or in the pursuit of self-interest.

Being aware of nuclear war and being able to imagine it and its alternative are not enough. Awareness is not always enough to motivate action. Several years ago when Harvard students were asked what probability they assigned to the likelihood of a nuclear war within the next ten years, most of them answered "ninety percent." Ninety-percent probable that there will soon be a nuclear war! And yet only five percent of them were active to avert this possibility. What discourages us from acting on the images that we've already entertained of Hiroshima, from further educating ourselves or talking about nuclear war to our friends, family and colleagues? What discourages us from joining a peace group and participating in its activities rather than just quieting the anxious God with a biannual check? What restrains us from making changes in our lifestyles, in our hierarchy of life-priorities, that would support a commitment to action to help avert nuclear war? Can we use imagination to help us understand this in order to act?

I believe we can, and I would like to turn to Schwartz's second way of putting the relationship we're looking at: responsibilities begin dreams. As we've seen, it can be images which awaken us to the evil of nuclear war. But once we are awakened, it is our responsibility—the necessity to respond, to act—which leads us back to the imagination to understand what holds us back from action.

II.

We recognize that much of thought is a conversation of voices—questioning, answering, criticizing, advising, praising, expressing. Our action depends on the orchestration of these voices, on which point of view, which character, is dominant at a given moment. Is it a "mothering one" who runs to soothe the other's anxiety, or a "working one" who longs for solitude in which he or she can become absorbed in a project, or is it a "fun-lover" who looks for ways to lighten, humor, enjoy? Often a single voice becomes so prevalent about an issue that it seems as though there is no other perspective, no second voice who objects or queries. At such moments, we say that one is "identified" with the first voice. To change habitual action or inaction, the relations among voices must shift.

For instance, let us take as an example an individual who becomes paralyzed around certain aspects of her work. We may find that within this person's depression she is the victim of a harsh voice who pinpoints with precision—and expresses with hyperbole—the nuances of inadequacy: "You never go far enough." "Your work always sounds shallow." "You're no good at this. You should give it up. It's a joke to continue." The ego voice may simply be overwhelmed, agree, and echo the critical voice, such that there sounds but one voice, a single point of view. In order to move from paralysis to action, one must begin to hear *in particular* what the voice says, what it is like, what its motives are. One must become aware of the process of "identification" and thereby regain a standpoint from which to hear the voice and eventually to dialogue with it. As one breaks the identification, one begins to take a more active role with respect to the voice—agreeing, disagreeing, acknowledging some criticism, but arguing, perhaps, for better-timed deliverance of the criticism—i.e., not at the inception of an action, where it will crush the action's future, but later, when pointing out a shallow part or a failure of logic will strengthen the work. How can we use these therapeutic insights regarding the voices of the imaginal—these insights which help us with our personal problems—to help us move toward action with regard to social problems, such as the prevention of nuclear war?

Lifton posits that each of us lives a "double life" with regard to nuclear war: one part of us doesn't want to hear about the possibility, defends itself through a state of *psychic numbness,* and goes about "business as usual"; while another part understands, and experiences feelingfully, that everything precious could be destroyed forever.[9]

If nothing else, the twentieth century should have taught us to keep a vigilant eye on "the numb one." For Wilhelm Reich, this is the one armored against feeling. Being "shut off from immediate contact with nature [and] people," the numb one acts with false pride, concerns himself with superficial appearances, engages in the banal, the ordinary.[10] For Reich, evil is none other than numbness. For Hannah Arendt, a student of the atrocities of our century, evil also takes on an ordinary face, the face of banality. Adolf Eichmann exemplified this for her. Unlike our usual notions of how evil people would seem, Eichmann was striking only in his "manifest shallowness." Though the "deeds were monstrous," the doer "was quite ordinary, commonplace, and neither demonic nor monstrous."[11] He presented himself with "clichés" and "stock phrases," "adhering to conventional, standardized codes of expression and conduct." He was not stupid but "thoughtless."[12] So if evil occurs in this mundane, ordinary way, then it is possible for all of us to perpetrate it—by sins of omission, by the actions we hold ourselves back from, as well as by sins of commission.

Grange Copeland, a Black character of the novelist Alice Walker, puts it this way to his granddaughter:

> "When I was a child," he said, "I used to cry if somebody killed an ant. As I look back on it now, I *liked* feeling that way. I don't *want*

to set here now *numb* to half the peoples in the world. I feel like something soft and warm an' delicate an' sort of *shy* has just been burned right out of me."

"Numbness is probably better than hate," said Ruth gently. She had never seen her grandfather so anguished.

"The trouble with numbness," said Grange, as if he'd thought it over for a long time, "is that it spreads to all your organs, mainly the heart. Pretty soon after I don't hear the white folks crying for help I don't hear the black."[13]

For the past three years I have met with small groups of people around our nuclear dilemma—both individuals who are inactive and those struggling to sustain or increase their anti-nuclear activism. We have met together to better understand this double life and to begin a dialogue between these voices within ourselves and our culture: the one who doesn't want to hear about nuclear war, the one who can't pretend she does not hear, and often a third, the one who can *act* to help avert nuclear war.

Just as in the example of a depressed person paralyzed around an aspect of work, the emphases have been on coming to know the voices who inhibit activism and those who sustain it, to work against an identification with a single voice, and to work toward a dialogue that allows one to move from a habitual stance of inaction or limited action. Let me caution. This effort has not been to eliminate one voice in favor of another, to kill off the numb part of one in partiality to the activist part. First of all, this proves impossible in the long run. The neglected or repressed voice always reasserts itself, often without our awareness. Secondly, as we shall see, some of the characters unconcerned about nuclear war can be valuable voices when their area of concern is circumscribed. It was the very tendency to isolate these voices we were trying to work against. When split, each presents itself simplistically, black or white, as polar opposites. Each voice sounds trite, stereotypic, uncomplicated, unsophisticated. When a dialogue can be sustained, each voice develops its point of view and becomes more internally complicated. It is less dismissive of the other and thereby less inhibitory.

I would like to share with you some of the imaginal background to activism and quiescence that we found. In groups whose members ranged in age from seventeen to sixty-five and which included students, professional and working people, we found an amazing confluence of imagery and characters among the 175 participants.[14] It is this commonality I would like to share with the hope of its striking a chord in you, that it might help you in your own action with respect to nuclear war (and other social problems as well).

We know that committing oneself to action is not achieved in a moment nor ever achieved once and for all. As with a commitment to another person, one comes up against doubts, frustrations, despairs, depressions, seemingly insolvable conflicts of interest. Both the path to becoming more active and the path of sustaining commitment to action require confrontations with the voices of denial, discouragement, belittlement, disillusionment—the voices who want the simpler life, the life of pleasure, the life of circumscribed pursuits.

Well, let's meet some of these voices—as we are sure to encounter them both in ourselves and in those we work and live with.

Let us begin with the one whose eyes skip over the column in the newspaper dealing with the installation of the MX; the one who flips the television channel as European protest against nuclear war becomes the topic; the one who does not want to think or feel about the possibility of nuclear war—the one who tropistically moves toward achieving a state of anaesthesia or numbness with regard to the topic of nuclear holocaust like a snail moves toward the safety and calm of its shell's darkness. The one who denies or minimizes the possibility of catastrophe and who clothes the images of Hiroshima in the statistics of survivability. The one who treats prophecies of nuclear war like weather predictions —possibly untrue and, if true, inevitable, leaving no recourse to human hands. The one who, like the citizens of Pompeii, goes about the business of planning life without figuring in this item of possible upset.

Who is this one who in seeming ignorance, naïveté, disinterest, preoccupation carries the evil of being benumbed, anaesthetized to the possible? Who is this one who tells us action is impossible? It will not make a difference.

I asked people to imagine this part of themselves as a character (like one in a short story or novel) and to find out what this character's world was like—what is important to him or her, what is the scene or setting of his or her activities? It would help you to understand their images if you shut your eyes for a moment and asked yourself the same questions: "What is that part of me like who hates sitting here reading a book on nuclear apocalypse, who does not want to have to act to avert nuclear war, whose interests and passions lie in other realms? Where does this one live? How does he or she spend an average day? What does he or she want a day to be like?"

It was possible to sort the kinds of figures who arose into six types of voices (neither exhaustive nor discrete)—six kinds of presences who benumb us to the reality of social problems, the immediacy of the nuclear danger. As I describe them, see if you can recognize each, in yourself, in the world.

Let's begin at the beginning with the character of the child—the child in us who is not immersed in the world of political daily events, but in the world of play. (Of course, actual children worry quite directly about nuclear war, but the imaginal child lives apart.) On one extreme is the child in nature, uncorrupted by the evils of society. When asked who inside of him doesn't want to hear about nuclear war, one thirty-year-old man saw a small, gentle, innocent boy, naked and vulnerable to the thoughtless whims of others. He lives in a dark, warm cave far above the city and society, on a mountainside in the wilderness, far away from the cruelties man inflicts upon his fellows. He avoids others, for contact with them is painful and frustrating. He'd rather be alone, living in harmony with nature and himself, allowing others to do what they may.

We meet another child down by a brook, on a bright summer day. She is eleven years old, lean and graceful with long golden hair. She plays with her friends, rides her horse through the meadows. She cannot comprehend what nuclear war means, what it is. She cannot imagine the possibility of her world being destroyed, for everything seems so peaceful, so completed.

Upon reflecting about this golden child, the woman who entertains her says that it is this innocent child who

blocks me from acting. It is the optimistic inability to comprehend the destruction of my world, the actual horror of the effects of nuclear war. When one part of me thinks it will happen, the child, in all her freshness, says it isn't possible.

Of course, there are other children too: the teenage boy who runs from one baseball game to the next, the spoiled little girl contained in the world of her own desires, and so on.

Besides the imaginal child's self-centeredness, absorption into the world of play and pleasures, besides her innocence and naïve belief in the continuation, the eternity of life, we confront the child's feelings of impotence, inability, and inadequacy within ourselves—the voice that stops our potential activism by saying "this problem is too complex, too big for me." "I don't know what to do about this. I wouldn't know where to begin." "My voice is too small. Nobody would hear me." There is an adult within who knows that, finally, there is no recourse to someone older and wiser to accomplish the things that must be done; that whether adequate to the task or not one must try, or it will never happen. The child within us stills this voice, leaving the tasks for someone older, more experienced to do.

Do you know what I mean? In this way, the child's innocence and youthfulness are potentially lethal, breeding as they do an evasion of responsibility, an evasion of trying to do whatever one *can* do.

The second type of numbing character is the worker in us, usually the specialist. For the worker, life is narrowed to the confines of the job. All else is experienced as unwelcome intrusion, interruption. The Worker moves very fast and efficiently, working long hours. He or she is absorbed—monomaniacally—in the task at hand. There are seldom people or family around. If there are, they are experienced as being in the way. The Worker's sense of self is sustained by the mastery of a specialized task in a circumscribed world. Let's meet a few of these workers.

A twenty-year-old woman, concerned about nuclear war but inactive, sees imaginally a janitor, busily cleaning up the daily messes of everyday life. He feels frustrated, angry. He is picking up rubbish in the auditorium. He is never there for the show, only afterwards, alone. He wants to be left alone to do his work, but he keeps hearing a voice over the intercom. He looks over his shoulder as though to tell this authority, this voice, to leave him alone, to stop bugging him and let him live his own life. He lives in a small, plain house in a uniform development.

Can you recognize this janitor? The one who cleans and tidies the mess of our daily life? Whose clean-up is never a prelude to getting started on a project? The one who makes a world of straightening the files, emptying the trash, watering the plants, arranging the chairs, balancing the checkbook; whose work is never done; who goes on repetitively each day re-cleaning, re-arranging the same rooms as yesterday? Can you feel how this one who tidies gets in the way of changing action? His job is never done. He pulls us to complete what is left unfinished, discourages us from starting something new that could increase the mess and further intrude upon the order he tries to set up.

A thirty-year-old woman sees another kind of "worker" character, Holly. Holly runs about frenetically all the time. In her twenties, Holly works as a computer personnel placement consultant for a Route 128 Boston firm. She loves everything fast, particularly cars. She lives with her husband and children in a prefab three-bedroom suburban ranch house, but this is not her life focus. She and her family rush past each other all the time, just as Holly rushes to and from work, and past people on her job. She's excited by the money she's making, the things she's able to buy, the deals she's able to take advantage of. For Holly, "profit" has utterly lost its original meaning, its meaning in the Bible and in Spinoza, of profit for the soul.[15]

Can we see Holly? The part of us on the ladder, moving up, excited by doing well at something, whether or not it means that much to us.

A different kind of "worker" character is the Scholar. The one who sits in his library, poring over leather-bound books, pondering specialized questions for long hours. His house is surrounded by a wall, cutting off the hubbub of the city beyond. He wants to be left alone; his project demands it. He works hard at what he does and believes he deserves his remove from the world. He is the one who tells us we must not take time from our pursuits to work on such things as nuclear war. We must stick to what we do well and leave world problems to others who are meant to work these things out. The importance of our projects and our dedication to them give us special dispensation.

The third type of character who benumbs us chooses isolation from the world of people to become surrounded by nature—most often he or she has "taken to the woods," which soon becomes a completed world. There is a dim awareness of outsiders' concerns about nuclear war, but nature soothes and comforts these concerns by its strength, continuity, massiveness. A mother of two imagines the numb aspect of herself as such a naturalist character, a rugged, individualistic woodsman. He lives alone with his animals in the woods and guides his life by the signs of nature. It is inconceivable to him that anything or anyone could destroy his world—it is too precious.

Another character is a woman who has moved to the woods with her children and husband because she wants to avoid hearing about nuclear war. She has no television or radio, and only slight contact with the townspeople to get supplies. She enjoys her isolation and detachment. She is healthy, hardy, cares well for her children. She hikes in the mountains, farms and cooks. Her main concerns are to live off the land and enjoy life. She writes every day for herself on matters that concern her.

As does a very strong and vital man who lives simply on an island in Maine, close to the earth and the sea. This character speaks to the imaginer, an activist professor with a long history of social concern. The only people who come to visit this character are other writers. They leave refreshed by the meeting.

Of course, we recognize these characters in the outer world as back-to-the-land people, as those individualists who will always struggle with their hermit-like proclivities, off on their own. But closer to home—amid the city as well—we can detect in ourselves a trend to isolation and detachment, an effort to take comfort in all that's natural (be it health food or flannel sheets) as a refuge against the atrocities and life-defeating technologies of the twentieth century . . . in, once again, an effort to live a circumscribed life, tending to the daily matters of sustaining life in the wilderness of modern times.

This isolation happens in the fourth type of character as well—the suburbanite. The world apart from one's own plot of neighborhood is a terrain to pass through—quickly on the commute, windows rolled up, doors locked, as much on the over- and underpasses of the superhighways as possible.

A twenty-five-year-old graduate student sees a character named

Jack building a brick wall. Jack proceeds methodically, one brick and then the next. As the wall gets taller, he sees a bomb blast in the distance. He picks up his supplies, moves to the other side of the wall, and continues to lay bricks. From here we see that this wall will surround his patio. He is looking forward to finishing so he can lie down on the chaise lounge with a beer and enjoy sitting in the sun with his wife on this gorgeous Saturday.

With their worries about mortgages, taxes, money-market funds, and their enjoyment of gardens and barbecue pits, the suburban characters carry that which is uniform, predictable, somewhat anonymous or stereotypic about our lives. The suburbanite neither gives himself over to work or hedonistic pleasures, but balances each in a circumscribed existence of family, work, and friends. This is the part of us that doesn't want to go too deep, doesn't want to give up the web of expectations that the mess of our lives hangs neatly upon. It is the part that does not want to make a move toward activism if that means moving out of the structure: secure job, pleasant home, average family. Let's face it, Levittown provides a residence for each of us psychically—pond sitter and urban dweller alike.

The fifth kind of character who doesn't want to think about nuclear war we'll call "the hedonist." Quite aware of the impending apocalypse but feeling powerless to avert it, he chooses to enjoy the moment. Time collapses into a pleasurable present. One is 'blissed out' on drugs, or nature, or the aesthetic pleasures of art, music, literature. Here we encounter the voice who says sarcastically that it doesn't matter what we do (live more frugally, join an anti-nuke group, give up aspects of professional or family life to devote oneself to social change). It simply doesn't matter, because life and the world are going to end anyway. One is reminded of the Germans in Hitler's bunker, dancing and drinking until the Russians came. (Or more contemporarily, one is reminded of the punk culture which has accepted the inevitability of annihilation and has set out to celebrate 'the end' in the present.) The only solution is to live now; buy the French meal, go to the Caribbean, make a bundle and retire early. "Go ahead, build a hot tub in the basement. The loan will never come due."

These characters embrace Thomas Hobbes's notion of happiness as the continuous progress from one greed to another. Their style of life is the radical hedonism Erich Fromm speaks about, where "the aim of life is happiness, that is maximum pleasure, defined as the satisfaction of any desire or subjective need a person may feel."[16] Not only is such hedonism a response to apocalyptic possibilities, but also as Fromm points out in *To Have or To Be,* it breeds war in its establishment of classes within and between nations, further dividing "the haves" and the "have nots."

There is a neighboring and last group of these characters whom we'll call the "gray lifers," who share the pessimism and sense of impotence of the hedonists. They too are confined to the present, not because they can enjoy its sweetness, but because the difficulties of the daily chain them there. Just surviving occupies their energies. These characters are buried with family and work responsibilities, struggles with money, and the drabness of their jobs and homes. These "gray lifers" are depressed, fearful, apathetic, dull. Unlike the "workers," they move slowly and do not enjoy their work. To take on thoughts about nuclear war would be one more burden. For some of them, the prospect of nuclear war is actually a relief, a final end to the hardness of daily life.

We find this one inside at those moments when to take up a cause seems too weighty. One is already exhausted, depleted, struggling to meet obligations, responsibilities. And now one is asked to go to more meetings, entertain more phone calls, more letters, more talk of depressing realities. This part of us, burdened down, loses a sense of life's beauty, of what is loved and treasured. When thinking of nuclear annihilation, this character borders on saying, "So what if it happens? No great loss." Or "It's what we deserve anyway." The thought of its happening confirms one's sense of life as desperate and unsalvageable.

If I have been successful in describing these to you, you will have been able to see most of these aspects working in your own relation to nuclear war. There is another way to hear these also, which has already crept in. That is, that we also find people who exemplify these voices, who have identified with one or another of them. Adults who speak with the naïve innocence and optimism of the child ("It will never happen") or with the child's inability to deal with the world of grownups ("Well, I don't know anything about politics or nuclear warfare, so I can't help on this"), people who confine themselves to the circumscribed world of their work, or who isolate themselves in the security of nature. Inside the consulting room one hears individuals who speak in the gray-lifer voice, who essentially say that life is so hard that nuclear devastation would put them out of their misery. Recently in *The New Yorker,* Lawrence Weschler described how Poles look forward to a nuclear war to solve some of their problems.[17] On the one hand, they magically feel when it happens it will not hit Poland. On the other, as one Polish woman put it, "But it's strange. Things are so bad that people here are almost longing for it"—longing for the devastation.

Let's change scenes now and turn to the characters who are not numb to the possibility of nuclear war, who are aware of it, think about it, and feel it. Again I asked people to let that part of themselves occur as a character in a book might: What would he or she be like, where would he or she live, what activities would he or she be engaged in? Ask yourself these same questions.

Once we meet the first group of these characters, we can better understand our eager identifications with the voices we have just heard. For these are alone, isolated in their despair, opened irreparably to the suffering coincident with nuclear war. One can see this in their eyes. In one description, blood streams down the face of a handsome blond character as he is strapped to the surface of a giant golden coin, arms and legs spread wide, stomach torn open. Blood streams down his face because his eyelids have been cut off—condemning him to constant sight, sight without the refuge of sleep or closed eyes. His open gut has been filled with every disease on earth. The coin turns over and over, as if it is being flipped by some giant hand beyond the man's control. Another character wanders blind, alone, crying. His eyes have been burnt blind by the horrific sights of postwar suffering.

The children are no longer playing in the meadows and the baseball fields. They are mongoloid, saddened, lost, wounded or deformed. No longer do they enjoy the protection of pursuing their own concerns and pleasures. As deformed children, they carry the awareness bred by wounds. One such child would have become a flower when looking at a flower if there were one around, but now in this postwar world she cries or moans, becoming the victims around her. Indeed, she embodies the Romantic notion of "sympathy"—of becoming the other. The rest of the children lie dead around a woman who is all alone, filled with anger at this sight of decaying, mangled and burnt bodies of children. These characters are far from numb. They stand immersed as victims in the images of destruction, as immobilized onlookers to the holocaust. They are passive, overwhelmed by emotion, despairing.

We are understandably afraid of this part of ourselves, which if led to focus on the possibility of nuclear war would lose itself to intense feelings of despair and depression. Anticipating this, Joanna Macy and others have provided "despair groups," places with other people at which one can contact these emotions and gradually go through them to a place of action to avert the holocaust.[18] When the despairing voice is repressed, Macy points out, one experiences a numbing of *all* affects, not just those concerning nuclear war.

This desperate group of characters, however, is not the only one aware of and responsive to the nuclear danger. The second we'll call "activists," though there are two distinct sides to this image. On one side we see "the peace activists" as young, hip, attractive, very busy people. They are confident, successful at movement work, enthusiastic about solving social issues. They've "got their heads together." Living in the city and surrounded by like-minded souls, they go to the museums and films, enjoying their awareness. There was a surprising uniformity about these characters, though—unlike the authors of the suburban characters described earlier—the imaginers failed to recognize such stereotypicality. Listening to these characters, I couldn't help but feel that their half-life was very short—limited as they seemed to be to youth.

On the other side we see a quite different group of inner activists: lonely, depressed, isolated, overworked characters. They, like the gray lifers, suffer through their responsibilities, without time for enjoyment or family and friends. Though at work in the city, they live in such places as a snow-covered mountain, above the tree line, with no shelter. These characters sacrifice themselves, without reward or certainty of success. They are pessimistic, non-escapists. One can see these characters as becoming increasingly depressed, burnt out, angry, bitter, although on the other hand they carry a kind of selfless dedication and awareness, a desire to persevere in spite of feelings of failure and inadequacy.[19] C. Wes Churchman, a student of world hunger, has stated that just such an active *acceptance* of oneself as a failure is critical to long-term commitment to social action.[20] Those who must succeed all the time cannot take on the tangle of a serious social problem.

The last class of such characters includes those who do not numb themselves to the possibility of nuclear war because of their love—their love of something in particular, which they wish to protect. In the previous group one doesn't know if the love of things has been covered by depression or whether the active struggle occurs more on the level of ideals, of the abstract.

For the present group, however, love and enjoyment of what is loved come first and motivate feeling and action. The loved objects are primarily the presence of nature and children. Within this group we find mother and teacher characters. The mothers come from various walks of life and, although activism is not their primary occupation, one senses renewable dedication, fed as they seem to be by concern for what is treasured.

III.

Well, what happens when the side of us who is numb and indifferent to the possibility of nuclear war meets with the side who recognizes, cognitively and affectively, the danger? I asked each participant in these groups to imagine and record a dialogue between the two characters who had arisen to them. This was done with the hypothesis that, if action can be supported or at least understood by both sides, if both sides can be taken into account when planning, then action will be less likely to be undermined or inhibited by a side of oneself.

What we found was that certain kinds of dialogue between these characters seemed destined to fail, end in stalemate, and result in further isolation of these two sides of ourselves. The most pervasive disaster in dialogue was the activist voice coming on piously self-righteous, indignant about the concerns and values of the numb one, unable to listen in the effort to preach—condescending, sarcastic, dismissive.

One character, a self-confident, energetic activist, stands over the bed of a "gray lifer," an exhausted one just trying to survive. She stands over the bedside singing exuberantly "Put on a Happy Face," "What the World Needs Now Is Love, Sweet Love," and "Amazing Grace." She tries to get the other one up, condemning her for her apathy. She does not speak to the depression and the exhaustion, but tries to override them entirely. We all know how successful this manner of approach is.

The encounter can move the other way also. The *un*concerned character, involved in her pregnancy and back-to-nature existence, tells her activist counterpart that she is making a big mistake doing this peace work. She should be getting married and having a family, but instead looks dowdy and overworked, never has any fun. And sometimes, of course, there is mutual derogation, back and forth, which leads to a quick "So long." Each lobbies to make the other become like herself, as though stubbornly sticking to her own position might succeed.

We are as familiar with these kinds of dialogue externally as we are internally. In fact, when discussing these modes of interacting, many participants recounted painful instances of being turned off to causes by the holier-than-thou approach of some activists. But now they could feel that tendency within and its roots in such things as disgust, frustration, disappointment and zealousness, in the fight of the active side not to be submerged by the pessimism, depression and self-interestedness of the other side.

But what kinds of rhetoric did work in these dialogues? What enabled the dialogue to be sustained, to be picked up again in the future, to not end in further alienation?

In one dialogue the character of a young mother who has entered the anti-nuclear movement to help protect her children meets a woman who has moved to the mountains. The latter says, "I find these nuclear issues quite distressing, and my husband and I have moved to the mountains to live our lives in solitude because of this problem." Instead of disparaging her for her escapism, the mother acknowledges that she too has thought of doing such a thing, as recently as several months ago. In joining the woman, she reduces the gap between them and is then able to share what made her stay—her fears for her children if legislation to fund the MX passes. The woman who has chosen solitude then confides that she doesn't think people have the power to change such decisions. The mother again empathizes with her point of view:

Mother: You know, I used to feel the same way; but we do have power to act as a whole.

> Country   Well, I do vote. But that's where my action stops. It's
> Dweller: such a hopeless situation to me.

At this point, something remarkable happens in the dialogue.
The mother *recognizes* her partner in dialogue. She realizes she
had seen her in Washington, D.C., in 1967, speaking against the
Vietnam war.

> Country   Yes, that was me. Perhaps. . . You remember that
> Dweller: day. . . . my friend with me had been killed that day by
>   the police. That was the end of my radicalism.

Do you hear what is amazing about this dialogue? Rather than
condemn this country dweller for her escapism, the mother
recognizes within herself some of the other woman's feelings, and
this in turn locates the activist within the one who escapes. And in
this location one is given direction for dialogue. The former activist
cannot just bounce into activity; she has feelings of loss, powerlessness and disillusionment to deal with. She could never be a
naïve activist, as she has already seen war.

Incidentally, in these dialogues no set of characters succeeds in
allowing and nurturing the movement of the numb character as
much as those who identified themselves as mothers or teachers.
Their usual tactics are either to find out what their partner in
dialogue treasures and appeal to them to protect that or to patient-
ly, very slowly introduce the other to the threat of nuclear war.[21]
This might be the part of us who begins getting us involved by
sharing "a little" reading for us to do—i.e., not demanding that we
become instantly involved.

In the failed dialogues, the supposedly more "feelingful" character takes the inactive one at face value—as indifferent, uncaring,
self-centered—and does not respond to hints of deeper feeling. For
instance, remember the character of the janitor, trying to do his job
while a voice over the intercom bothers him? It turns out to be the
voice of another character, a determined, powerful young woman
on her way to a rally against nuclear weapons.

> Janitor: Why don't you leave me alone? I just want to go on
>   with my work.

Young Woman:	You're just going to go about your business and leave the work to us?
Janitor:	I don't want to know.
Young Woman:	I feel like just walking out on you because there's no communication. Do I have to pull you out the door of this auditorium and push you into the middle of the rally's crowd outside?
Janitor:	I'm doing my work. Can't you see? And when I come home I want to find meaning. I can't deal with doing this job and at the same time feeling a pile of jigsaw pieces in my stomach.
Young Woman:	You've got to put away your other self and *be* that part who wants to change things.
Janitor:	I am too out of touch with that part. It's buried under some floor boards deep inside. He's pushing to get up, but I don't want to see him.

Instead of asking about the jigsaw pieces in his stomach or about the one pushing up on the floor boards, the young woman terminates the conversation. She misses attending to his clues that his indifference is not simple-minded, but complex—it is not what it seems. Through his manic, repetitive work, he tries unsuccessfully to nail down the floor boards. She needn't "walk out on him because there is no communication" or tell him what she would do if she were him; she could simply focus him on those floor boards.

In some dialogues it was possible for the activist one to recognize and draw on the strengths of the more detached character. The ability to circumscribe a manageable area in which to work and succeed may be a natural instinct to the numb one which the activist badly needs in order not to be overwhelmed by the immensity of the problem. Let me give you an example:

Billy, a character who is a copyboy in a newsroom, is upset about nuclear war but is not a strong newswriter. He usually runs maniacally from one assignment to the next. He goes to visit the strong, vital man who lives simply on an island in Maine, close to the earth and sea. Though not an activist himself, he is willing to talk about war when Billy brings it up. He inspires Billy to write a set of relevant columns and, perhaps as importantly, gets him to do a little fishing before he goes back to the mainland.

Indeed, this invitation "to do a little fishing" seems critical in some of the dialogues. Particularly the isolated, overworked activist and the despairing one with eyes fixed open could use "a little fishing." As a psychic alternative, fully identifying with these characters would seem to have a very short future. I am reminded of Robert Coles's piece "Social Struggle and Weariness" written during the Civil Rights movement in the South, where such isolated and despairing souls would burn out.[22] Battle symptoms of exhaustion, weariness, despair, frustration and rage would often precede either leaving the movement altogether or becoming "troublesome, bitter, and a source of worry, of unpredictable action, of potential danger to themselves and their 'cause'."[23]

Indeed, in studying why individuals leave movements—for civil rights or peace—one finds that the first set of voices has asserted itself strongly—the one who wants to enjoy the pleasures of a profession, of a family, or of a more middle-class existence. The individual who leaves a movement is often tired of fighting against "big problems," a struggle in which one never fully succeeds, and often feels as though things are worsening despite devoting so much time and energy and sacrificing so much of what life offers. One longs for the more circumscribed existence enjoyed by former friends, who can experience both pleasures and successes, who can feel effective within a narrower world. These findings would suggest to those of you who are very active in the anti-nuclear movement that dialogue with the first set of voices is as critical to sustaining one's commitment to action over the long haul as listening to the second set of voices is important for others in becoming more active.

As Jonathan Schell points out in *The Fate of the Earth,* "As far as we can tell, there will never again be a time when self-extinction is beyond the reach of our species."[24] This fact has a consequence for the shape of our activism. Peace activism can no longer be largely relegated to periods of tension, war or possible war. It must be ongoing, ever vigilant, no matter what gains are made in its favor. This means that we must nurture a lifelong commitment to action to promote peace—not just a commitment for our "student years" or our "retirement years," but during the rest of our life, amidst our busy-ness with other things.

I have suggested that one way of supporting such action is to be aware of those voices in thought that surround our attempts at action. It is such dialogue that Hannah Arendt speaks about as a way to overcome the "thoughtlessness" of our own Eichmann-like tendencies. She reminds us that for Socrates thought is an internal dialogue. In the *Hippias Major,* Socrates says that when Hippias, "an especially thickheaded partner . . . goes home, he remains one [single], for though he lives alone, he does not seek to keep himself company. He certainly does not lose consciousness; he is simply not in the habit of actualizing it."[25] Hippias does not think about his deeds; he holds no inner dialogue. When Socrates goes home, however, he is met by a voice: "a very obnoxious fellow who always cross-examines him," whom Socrates describes "as a very close relative [who] lives in the same house."[26] Socrates wants to come to some agreement with this relative—to become friends with this voice—because, after all, they must live under the same roof. Hippias avoids this voice by ceasing to think, by not opening the dialogue. Arendt elaborates Socrates' example:

> [the] criterion for action will not be the usual rules, recognized by multitudes and agreed upon by society, but whether I shall be able to live with myself in peace when the time has come to think about my deeds and words.[27]

If we follow this logic, one form of moral imagining would be to open ourselves consciously to the kinds of dialogues I have described around nuclear war; to allow the sides to challenge and contradict each other; to stick with them as they find a way of living with each other; and, most importantly, to follow the path of action that their dialogue points to.

1.   Elise Boulding, Warren Ziegler and others have been extending Fred Polak's theory of "the image of the future" to our present planetary crisis. Briefly, group participants are asked first to imagine a world without weapons thirty years hence. Second, they are asked to work backwards from this utopic image and describe (as a historian might) events at each five-year period from the future image to the present reality, i.e., events that would have to happen if the more ideal future image were to eventuate.

This last step is critical, for as Hirschman has pointed out, utopic imagining alone can lead to the breakdown of the very vision it promulgates. Activists who have been unable to imagine *intermediate* visions of society experience continual disappointment and frustration because of the gap between imagination and reality. These feelings of despair and discouragement can lead to abandonment of a movement, and a turn in the culture from a period of public action to one of private interest. Cf. Elise Boulding, "The Social Imagination and the Crisis of Human Futures: A North American Perspective," *Forum for Correspondence and Contact* 13/2 (1983): 43–56; F. Polak, *The Image of the Future,* trans. E. Boulding (New York: Oceana Press, 1961); A. O. Hirschman, *Shifting Involvements: Private Interest and Public Action* (Princeton: Princeton University Press, 1982).

2.   See M. J. Carey, "Psychological Fallout," *Bulletin of the Atomic Scientists* 38 (January 1982): 20–24. For a summary of this work, see also R. J. Lifton, *The Broken Connection* (New York: Simon & Schuster [Touchstone], 1980).

3.   Quoted in P. Ball, *The Central Self: A Study in Romantic and Victorian Imagination* (London: Athlone Press, 1968), p. 14.

4.   W. J. Bate, "The Sympathetic Imagination in Eighteenth-Century English Criticism," *English Literary History* 11 (1945): 149.

5.   Quoted in ibid., p. 144. One reason for the harshness of the Romantics' critics was that their claims were so vast for imagination as to be considered indiscriminate.

6.   J. Engell, *The Creative Imagination* (New York: Harvard University Press, 1981), pp. 8, 243.

7.   T. A. Repina, "Development of Imagination," in *Psychology of Preschool Children,* ed. A. Zaporozhets and D. B. Elkonin (Cambridge: MIT Press, 1971).

8.   D. Moss, "The Erotics of Destruction" (Presented at The American Orthopsychiatric Association Symposium, "Dealing with Plans for the Annihilation of Life on Earth: The Reality of the Arms Race," Boston, April 4–8, 1983).

9.   R. J. Lifton, "Psychological Effects of Nuclear Weapons and Nuclear War," in *Proceedings of Harvard Medical School Conference: The Medical Consequences of Nuclear Weapons and Nuclear War* (Cambridge, Massachusetts, 1981).

10.   W. Reich, *Ether, God and Devil* (New York: Farrar, Straus and Giroux, 1973), p. 124.

11.   H. Arendt, *The Life of the Mind* (New York: Harcourt Brace Jovanovich, 1978), p. 4.

12.   Ibid.

13.   D. Bradley, "Novelist Alice Walker, Telling the Black Woman's Story," *New York Times Magazine,* 8 January 1984, p. 27.

14.   Each group met only once for one to three hours, depending on circumstance. With a few exceptions the participants had no training for imagery work, and yet each was able to experience the presence of these voices. The descriptions of these characters are drawn from participants' written reports.

Those familiar with imaginal characters will note that they are in the beginning stages of character development, often lacking the depth and complexity of voices one has entertained in imagination over time. Nevertheless, it is their very closeness to consciousness that allows us so easily to recognize them in our daily actions and attitudes.

15. E. Fromm, *To Have or To Be* (New York: Bantam Books, 1981), p. xxvi.

16. Ibid., pp. xxv–xxvii.

17. L. Weschler, "A Reporter at Large (Poland–Part II)," *The New Yorker,* 18 April 1983, p. 10.

18. J. Macy, "Despair Work," *Evolutionary Blues* (Summer/Fall, 1981); and Macy, *Despair and Personal Power in the Nuclear Age* (Philadelphia: New Society Publishers, 1983).

19. Both images of the activist suggest the critical need to broaden and deepen our perceptions and images regarding action. The range of action participants imagined was narrow, mainly limited to demonstrating and organizing. Even the images in these two categories lacked specificity.

20. C. W. Churchman, Lectures at the Wright Institute, San Francisco, California, Summer 1981.

21. It is interesting that all the individuals who entertained this kind of character (mother and teacher characters) were women. This finding, however, must be seen in conjunction with another. Whereas over half of the women in these small groups imagined one or more of their characters as a male, not a single male spontaneously entertained a female character. Many men may indeed be cut off from the feminine voices in dealing with "the numb one."

22. R. Coles, "Social Struggle and Weariness," *Psychiatry* 27 (1964): 305–15.

23. Ibid., p. 308.

24. J. Schell, *The Fate of the Earth* (New York: Avon Books, 1982), p. 55.

25. Quoted in Arendt, *Life of the Mind,* p. 188.

26. Ibid.

27. Ibid., p. 191.

Additional References

Keniston, K. *The Uncommitted.* New York: Harcourt, Brace & World, Inc., 1965.

Mack, J. "Psychosocial Effects of the Nuclear Arms Race." *The Bulletin of the Atomic Scientists* (1981): 18–23.

WOLFGANG GIEGERICH

Wolfgang Giegerich is a training analyst, political thinker and lecturer at the C. G. Jung Institute in Stuttgart, as well as the Eranos Conferences, Ascona, Switzerland. Dr. Giegerich received his university training in Wurzburg and Göttingen, Germany, and Berkeley, California. He was assistant professor of German literature at Rutgers University from 1969–1972. He is now editor of *Gorgo,* a journal which delves into the meaning of terrorism and the current ecological crisis, linking these subjects to the imagination and to the loss of soul. He has just completed writing a major book called *Psychoanalysis of the Nuclear Bomb.*

Saving the Nuclear Bomb

Let me admit right at the outset that "Saving the Nuclear Bomb" sounds perverse. For after all, is it the nuclear bomb that is threatened and needs to be saved, or is it not much rather *we,* who have to be saved from its threat? To want to save the nuclear bomb means turning things upside down. This is how it looks at first glance. But let us not be too hasty. Perhaps there is a sense in which it is indeed the bomb that is threatened, so that it would be legitimate to try to rescue, preserve, and redeem it. Then, of course, "saving" could not stand for the unscrupulous production of nuclear weapons and for protecting them against any word of warning or call for moderation and reflection. "Saving" would have to mean something altogether different.

That which threatens the bomb is our general frame of mind, the way we meet reality, especially when it is undesirable. It seems that Western man has only two approaches to reality, two ways to deal with predicaments. The one approach is the call for the expert who, with his knowledge of the facts and his technological know-how, has to find a way out, a method of how to get rid of the problem—how to cut the tumor out or bombard it with rays, how to safely dump poisonous waste, how to free us from crime, exterminate insect pests or human enemy forces. The other approach is the personal feeling reaction and the call for political action. We are for or against armament, abortion, evolution or what have you; we demonstrate in the streets, sign petitions, protest with clenched fists, demand that this (or the opposite) be done.

In neither case is the phenomenon causing us concern seen for what it is. To be sure, the mind of the expert looks objectively at

the facts, but only with a view to ridding us of the problem, to doing away with it. It is an exterminating, dumping frame of mind:
pesticides, antibiotics and the like are its trademark. But I want to
stress that I am not just talking of the actual physical elimination of
problems, but much rather of the prior and more subtle extermination in our way of thinking about them, in the sense that unwelcome things are looked at exclusively as problems to be done away
with. The same applies to the second, the pro or con approach to
reality. Paradoxically, when we demonstrate, let's say, for or
against the bomb, the bomb itself is not the important thing, but
what really counts and what we really demonstrate is *our* personal
feelings about it, our wishes. We are displaying ourselves, talking
more or less autistically about ourselves, whereas the bomb, as a
real phenomenon in its own right, is not much more than a peg for
the manifestation of our emotions or opinions, our pro or con. So
here too the real phenomenon is discarded, dumped.

In fairy tales, when the hero or heroine is in distress, he often
comes across a brook which murmurs something to him/her, a
tree, a bird, the wind which gives some important piece of advice,
a frog, a horse, a snake which demands some service. Animals and
things were able to speak. Why do animals, trees, and things not
speak to us? It is because such speaking belongs solely in the world
of fairy tales, but not in the real world; solely in the age once-
upon-a-time, but not in the here and now? I do not think so.
Nature speaking is not, or would not have to be, a mere fairytale
motif, a miracle, an utterly unreal fiction. Things do speak even
today. Only, with our problem-solving mentality, we do not hear,
we refuse to listen. And of all things, it is particularly the nuclear
bomb that is speaking to us today. Indeed, it is not merely mur-
muring like the fairytale brook or whispering like the wind. It is
yelling, shrieking, louder and louder, becoming ever more extreme, so that we need more and more noise, twenty-four-hour
television, disco music, the loudness of high feelings or, on the
other hand, perhaps something like the deafening silence of
meditation to block out the voice of reality. Because there is no ear
to listen to the message that real things have to impart, reality may
well have to work itself up to its last resort, to the din of a nuclear
explosion—to at least make itself felt, if not heard.

We really do not hear. We do not even know what hearing could
possibly mean in this context. It is absolutely out of the question

for us that such a thing as the bomb might have a message for us, could be a source of insight or even of wisdom. We know that things do not speak. They are dumb. Only man speaks and has an intelligence. Things, plants, animals are there to be used, to be disposed of.

But the nuclear bomb is something so utterly incredible and terrible that disposing of it one way or another just won't do. You can't get rid of something real. You could at best exchange one evil for another, usually worse. No matter whether we build more and better bombs—or, conversely, eliminate them all—the bomb itself as a reality, as a powerful idea, would remain, and remain unseen. So saving the nuclear bomb has nothing to do with defending it against the peace movement, but it means a third way beyond the entire alternative of pro or con, war or peace. It means listening to its voice, seeing its face, acknowledging its reality, and releasing it into its own essence. It means saving it from our habitual throwaway mentality. The question is not how to dispose of the bomb, but where to pose it, where to find its legitimate place.

I am here transferring the depth-psychological attitude toward the individual person's symptom to the way of looking at the symptom of the body politic. C. G. Jung once said that in our "neurosis is hidden our best enemy or friend."[1] He did not just say friend. He said enemy *or* friend. Put this way, friend and enemy cancel each other out, showing that the entire category of friend or enemy, pro or con, the perspective of our human likes and dislikes becomes irrelevant. What remains is "our best (friend or enemy)"—our best, that is to say, the dignity of the real phenomenon itself, independent of, and prior to, our subjective valuation, a dignity even if the phenomenon is as painful as a neurotic symptom or as dangerous, if not as evil, as the nuclear bomb. "Saving" means to restore the dignity of things.

Because of our century-long training in quelling the voice of reality, we are not right away in a position from where we could hear the nuclear bomb speak or see its face. We have to overcome long distances to get there. And all I can hope to do in this remaining half hour is to move us to a point where—if we are not too much out of breath—we at least can have a glimpse of its countenance, an inkling of its message. I will approach this point in a roundabout way, by leaving the bomb aside for the time being and turning first to another subject: nature.

In former times, nature was a wilderness, surrounding man on all sides, infinitely superior and inexhaustible. Human settlement, by contrast, was merely a tiny island within it. Nowadays this relationship is increasingly being reversed. It is nature that is about to become insular and to withdraw into the "zoo" or into that expanded version of the zoo we call nature reserve, wildlife sanctuary or national park, whereas the world of civilized mankind is more and more becoming the all-encompassing framework. This is not merely a quantitative change, the spreading of habitation and civilization and the corresponding diminishment of virginal nature. It is something much more radical than the fact that wilderness is merely being pushed back to a few remnants. This is only the measurable aspect of what has taken place. But along with this quantitative reduction of wild nature to a few islands, a less noticeable but nevertheless world-shaking qualitative change is going on: a reversal in the relationship of nature and man, and thus a fundamental transformation in the very *notion* of nature, in its ontological essence, in what "nature" means.

It used to be inherent in the notion of nature that it is that which encompasses and bears our existence. Nature, that was Mother Earth, who brings forth and nourishes man and also takes him in again at his death. But what is nature today? She is no longer Mother, but rather man's problem child. Now man is called upon to accept responsibility for nature, indeed to guarantee her survival—wildlife conservation, environmental protection. It is as if nature had become senile and helpless and now were utterly dependent on the care of her grown-up children, or as if she were on welfare requiring our planning and support.

Strictly speaking, wildlife conservation or nature protection is a contradiction in terms. For in the very moment that nature needs to be protected, it is no longer nature in the true sense, and thus it is precisely by way of the protection of nature that its ontological annihilation is taking place, nature's denaturation.

The change from the Great Mother to the problem child strikingly reveals the reversal that has taken place. Of course, you might say, nature needs protection only because we ruthlessly exploited the wilderness in the first place. But that we were able to do this is the very point. In former times, man could have committed the worst sin against nature without doing her any real harm; she would always have remained infinitely superior to him. But now the fate of nature herself is given into the hands of man. In this sense, it is now we who are superior to her and surround her from all sides.

We can express this change also as a movement from one place or *topos* to another. In earlier times, the place of nature was the open expanse surrounding man. My word for nature when it is at this *topos* is "wilderness." The other *topos* I term "zoo." In the zoo, the animals that used to belong to the wild are now locked into cages, so that they cannot threaten us from without. Rather, we can now in all safety walk around them. If "zoo" is here understood, not as an empirical locality, but rather as an ontological *topos,* a place in the imagination, then "zoo" means that *topos* at which wild nature is encircled by and embedded in the civilized world. Zoo means that ontological place at which nature—quite unnaturally—has its essence in being the object of human caretaking, planning, and research. Thus we find the zoo in this sense even where there is no literal zoological garden, not even a nature reserve, but where animals can still be seen in the wild. For even these animals have long ago become the objects of the curiosity of television viewers or of the cameras of safari tourists. At bottom, therefore, they are once and for all animals of the zoo, fenced in by the bars of an imaginal cage that modern man carries with him in his mind even when he ventures into the last remains of virginal nature. And his camera is the outward token and replica of the imaginal chamber—"camera"—into which all nature is placed today. With every photograph we prove our power to capture nature in a box that we can carry around with us, the power to freeze it onto film.

The same world-shaking change that happened to nature can also be observed with respect to history. Here too there is a reversal from a wide expanse or "wilderness," in which man found himself, to a tame interior, into which history is fenced. This interior is the museum, history's equivalent of the zoo of nature. More and more the museum is becoming the place of history. Everything historical moves into the museum and turns into an antique. It is torn out of the "wilderness," that is out of its living tradition and customary use, and is imprisoned in showcases, where we can safely walk around it. I say safely, for in former times the objects that we now find in the museum might, as it were, have "assaulted" us much as did certain wild animals. Let us take an altarpiece as an example. In the museum, the painting is the dead object of the tourist's aesthetic contemplation or curiosity. The same painting in its original place in the church a few hundred years ago would have "assaulted" the believer with its demand to bend his knees before it and cross himself in devotion. There the picture was alive; it had a will of its own.

Of course, just as with the "zoo," the "museum" does not refer solely to the literal building or institution of that name, but is the term of an imaginal *topos*. For even cathedrals and entire medieval cities that on account of their size would not fit into a museum are nonetheless huge open-air museums; and historical personages, events or movements—which, since they are immaterial, could not be shown in a museum—are being viewed with a museum frame of mind.

Just as nature is to be protected, so the relics of history, when seen from the museum point of view, must be preserved and restored—protection of historical monuments. History too has been ontologically annihilated and denatured because it is deprived of its innermost nature, which was to be the wind of time. It has been reduced to a mass of antiques and factual knowledge about the past, a mass that has to be collected and protected by us. Here, too, man has taken over the responsibility for the historical and stands no longer *in* history, exposed to its wind. History has likewise become insular, so to speak, captured and contained in the museum, the history book, or in the documentary, not to mention in Disneyland.

Fortunately, we can observe a little more closely the actual historical moment of the radical reversal from man's embeddedness in something expansive surrounding him to a state where that which used to surround him has shrunk to a limited object now encircled by man. I want to show this in one small example: in the change from the fear exuding for seventeenth-century man from the terrors of night, of thunderstorms, and of high mountains to eighteenth-century man's beginning fascination with the horrible. Way into the seventeenth century, it was generally customary that every night before going to bed the head of the house would gather the entire household around him to say prayers for the night. Single people would sing their evening hymn in their bed chamber. We still have copies of the prayer and hymn books that people used then and that were produced and reprinted in millions of copies. They were true bestsellers of their age, which shows that they expressed and responded to the actual feelings of the vast majority of people. Now, the texts of these evening prayers abound in descriptions of the horrors of the night. Some of them refer to actual, even if rather unlikely, dangers that might befall the innocent sleeper—such as fire, theft, murder, or the violation of the virgin during her sleep. For the most part, however, they are monotonous clichés about totally unspecific dangers, the terror, awe and fear coming with the night, "black, sinister night." As Richard Alewyn, who wrote about these fears, said, it is precisely the monotony of these clichéd descriptions that is evidence of their authenticity.[2] Obviously, these are fears of intangible dangers of the night that cannot be pinned down to anything empirical, fears of the imaginal or mythical horrors of the night.

Similarly, the rugged mountains of the Alps caused sheer terror in the people of that age. The very same sights that today attract millions of tourists were then experienced as horrifying. Even courageous men would not venture into the "desolate and wayless wilderness of forests and mountains" without necessity. In the reports of travelers to Italy who had to cross the Alps, we read how horror-stricken they were at the sight of gorges and cliffs.

A hundred years later the situation began to change as a result of the Enlightenment. I confine myself to one example that I also owe to a paper by Alewyn. Jean Jacques Rousseau, the French philosopher, describes in his autobiography that he loved to walk to his favorite place in the Savoyan Alps, a path at the edge of a ravine where, secured by a railing, he could look down into the gorge in order *"de gagner des vertiges tout à mon aise"* (to procure the feeling of dizziness for himself at his ease), and he adds, "I love this whirling, provided that I am in safety."[3]

Let us dwell for a moment on this image of Rousseau leaning on a railing and looking down into the gorge. What does this image tell us? What change has taken place here so that the same gorge that might have struck seventeenth-century man with horror could now become thrilling?

I said, the same gorge. Indeed, the Alps out there did not change. What changed was the ontological framework within which the same sight is seen and from which it receives its nature, its ontological quality and status. In the one case, in the earlier century, the ravine was, to be sure, just as limited as at the time of

Rousseau. But obviously, it was not confined to being merely this one particular thing. Rather, it opened up and allowed you to see the abyss of being as such, the primordial void, the yawning chasm prior to all creation, cosmological Chaos. The one individual gorge was like a window through which all-encompassing wilderness was glaring at you and into your life, threatening to intrude into the insular human world of day, hope, and safety. You looked at this particular thing, the one ravine there, but what you saw in it was all around you, also behind your back and even in your own heart. And thus you were in it; your safety was only the borrowed security of a small boat on the ocean of being. It would have been impossible during that age to put a fence around the ravine, because despite its limited quantitative size, it was immense, endless, bottomless.

Rousseau, on the other hand, is truly safe. As he is looking down into the gorge, he knows that the danger is only in front of him right there, whereas from all other sides he is secure. The gorge is not threatening him from behind, as it would have been in the earlier age. Rousseau lives in the state of salvation, we might say. And it is only because he is *backed up* by the fundamental security of the civilized world that he can without terror look at this particular instance of danger and even enjoy the thrill of it. If we imagine that Rousseau's favorite place had been a round crater instead of a narrow ravine, he might have walked all round it. Or, if we transpose this scene into our time, we might imagine, on a nice summer Sunday, hundreds of tourists, each having the total safety of human civilization and rationality at their backs, standing all around and staring down into the spectacular depth. Rousseau was looking into the gorge all alone, but potentially it is mankind at large that now has surrounded the danger, and Rousseau is here just its one exchangeable representative.

Here we can actually see the new ontological situation. The wild is no longer the open expanse all around us, but it is a small spot encircled by and embedded in human civilization. Now there is a railing. Now chaos can be fenced in, enclosed, captured behind the bars of a cage, bottled and encapsulated; and as such it can be used in small calculated doses *within,* and *for the benefit of,* the human world of ego-consciousness and rational civilization, as a stimulant and source of tourist excitement or spare time entertainment.

The once infinite, bottomless expanse of the wild, to which

human existence was exposed and in which it was completely contained, has been shoved, as it were, from "out there" over Rousseau's railing into the fenced-in area to be confined there. It is now within, incorporated and interiorized by man. The ravine has been narrowed down to a finite positive thing, an empirical object, a particular ($τόδε\ τι$, in Aristotelean terminology), when once it had been a *topos,* a world, the world of terror. And this terror has been taken away from the real ravine; it has ceased being an objective quality of reality—ontological, cosmological, or mythical—and has turned into a mere human feeling, a subjective state *in* man, the dizziness or thrill in Rousseau or the pathological fear in the neurotic. Here we can witness the transition from an existence grounded in the imagination to an existence in positivism, in a world pieced together from things each locked into themselves, firmly encircled by the fence of the human-all-too-human.

I spoke of the seventeenth-century evening prayers. Night after night millions of people repeated the same statements of terror. We might think that this was a kind of collective anxiety neurosis or that these people were uncommonly fearful. But the opposite is the case. First, they were not talking about their *own* fears, but about the horrors *of the night.* Secondly, they were not running away in fear and trembling from any dangers, imagined or real, but on the contrary felt the need daily to *evoke* the terrors of night and to give to them a real presence in their lives. Their prayers actually were a devoted incantation, a conjuring up of images of horror. And with these images they went to bed. So what actually happened was that they *bedded* themselves in the terror of night. And precisely because of this, I think, they presumably had a sound sleep—as incredible as it may sound to our modern ears.

For we have turned things outside in. We think that the beginning and foundation of existence must be safety, secure rationality, primal trust, love and peace and that all anxiety or feeling of insecurity or irrationality must certainly be due to some accident or mistake, a mother who did not love enough (or who loved too much), or some such thing. Terror, irrational chaos, bottomless depth cannot be the ground and the source of existence. They must certainly, we think, originate merely in some malfunction, error or sin *within* the already created world, within ourselves, or family constellation or the structure of human society.

But, I submit, there is an immediate connection between the oft-cited alienation and uprootedness of modern man and his belief that he must be embedded in security and salvation and not in the terrors of night. For here, human existence is burdened, and over-burdened, with the task of being its own ground and thus is deprived of some Other in which it could be rooted. And converse-ly, I submit, it is when existence is embedded in terror, in the irra-tional bottomless depth of being, that man is made to feel at home on the earth.

From here I would like to return to the nuclear bomb. When it was acknowledged that terror and wilderness surround us on all sides, this had the advantage that one could let go of one's anx-ieties, fears, and insecurity. Certainly they were there, but they were also released into the immense open expanse of the wild and did not have to be personally ours. When, however, we insist that the imaginal terror or the terror of the imaginal be confined in par-ticular things and be fenced in within the all-surrounding security of the rational human world, then this has two consequences. On the one hand, all subjective feelings of anxiety will be locked into the personality, causing all kinds of neurotic conditions there. And on the other hand, the truly, objectively terrible will have to appear as an empirical, literal reality. In order to establish a truly safe and rational world as the *foundation* of existence—that is, in order to bring salvation to the world and to man—everything irrational had to be shoved one by one from the endless wilderness around us to an interior encircled by us. The labor and process of moving the irrational from "out there" around us to "in here" is called science, scientific progress. It is the move from the imaginal to our positivistic reality.

For just this could be the definition of the imaginal: to be the state of being "out there around us," all over the place; and the definition of the positively real: to be the state of being "in here," this one thing only, this problem. The more that irrational terror is captured in the safe container of some interior, behind a fence or in a shell or in a clearly defined "problem," the more concentrated and literal—that is, physical—the terror will become. More and more terror has to be packed into concrete things that we can han-dle according to our schemes, if the realm of freedom from the ter-ror surrounding us is to be enlarged. The utmost result to date of this endeavor (to create a world of salvation no longer embedded in and thus exposed to terror) is the nuclear bomb, into and behind whose shell has been collected and concentrated all the terror that previously had been *spread out* all over the world.

But in the nuclear bomb the reversal reverses itself and the repressed returns. For so much terror, so much irrationality has been crammed into the nuclear bomb that it is full to the bursting point. And even though it is a relatively small and safe thing at our disposal, it nevertheless threatens us again *as if from without,* inasmuch as it puts human existence, and indeed the existence of our entire planet, on the razor's edge. It was the counterphobic crusade against the imaginal terror that itself produced the first *literally* existing terror—the very real possibility of an actual and total apocalypse.

What is the bomb? It is the wild in its modern guise, our twentieth-century version of all-encompassing wilderness, its last remnant. Encapsulated, to be sure, into a tiny, manageable shell, and tangible indeed, it is nonetheless the very wilderness of old in a different shape—no longer out there, i.e., in nature, but in here, i.e., in technology. Thus it is the only place left today where we can authentically house and deposit our anxiety. It is our last *genuine* and *real* connection to something bigger and more powerful than we. And what is the face staring at us from within the bomb? Ultimately, it is the face of the dark God, *deus absconditus, mysterium tremendum,* described in Exodus 23: 27 and elsewhere as the true terrorist: *"terrorem meum mittam in praecursum tuum"* (I will send my terror before you).

So, should we ban the bomb, get rid of it? Or make use of it as a weapon? In either case we would miss our chance. I think we should save it and neither try to destroy it nor to waste it in a one-time explosion, through which it would go up in smoke, and ourselves along with it. I would suggest that we ground our existence in it, dwell near it, make our home in it. For in fact, it already *is* our home; our existence already is bedded on thousands of warheads. Therefore my suggestion to ground ourselves in the nuclear bomb is not as outrageous as it may sound. It merely amounts to tuning in to our reality, to acknowledging the embeddedness that already is, to putting our heart into what we (as mankind) have been and are doing *anyway,* whether we personally like it or not. We must stop fooling ourselves by thinking we could be against a thing, while at the same time producing it. And there must be an end to the counterphobic move, which brings forth precisely that from which it would free us.

We have to realize that the nuclear bomb is not just a fluke of history, an unfortunate by-product of science, but that it is the epitome and culmination of science, the product of modern man's highest and most sacred aspirations, his search for the ultimate forces of being, and for salvation. In the nuclear bomb is invested the soul of modern man, in it *"habemus animam nostram."* An entire world, the most supreme, the utmost in the way of essence, substance, and worth, has been packed into it. And only for this reason does the nuclear bomb have the power to annihilate the world. For if what is in it were vain and idle, it would not possess any reality and thus could not do much harm. To modify a Latin saying: *Nemo contra mundum nisi deus ipse* (Nothing can destroy the world but God himself). I say this of course not to deny the destructive power of the seemingly man-made nuclear bomb, but to help us recognize what this destructive power of the bomb actually *is*.

Are you suffering from the loss of meaning? Searching for a spiritual dimension? Wanting to reconnect to the imagination? Longing for a God, a fate, an unprogrammed future? Don't go to India, nor back to classical or primitive mythology, nor off into drugs nor into yourself. Go to *our* reality, try the *real* thing: try the nuclear bomb. All the riches of the imaginal that we think we have lost are there, stuffed away and buried and hidden, but also preserved in its terror, waiting to be redeemed.

1.   I am quoting directly from the German original (*GW* 10, §359) in my own translation, since the official translation in the *Collected Works*, by making the statement sound more 'logical,' loses the subtlety of the paradox expressed by Jung.

2.   R. Alewyn, "Die Lust an der Angst," in *Probleme und Gestalten: Essays* (Frankfurt a.M.: Insel, 1974), pp. 307–34.

3.   "J'aime beaucoup ce tournoiement, pourvu que je sois en sûreté." Jean Jacques Rousseau, *Oeuvres Complètes* (Bibliothèque de Pleiade, Librairie Gallimard, 1959), vol. 1, p. 173 (near the end of book 4).

DANILO DOLCI

Poet, architect, educator and social reformer, Danilo Dolci is a world leader in non-violent action. He received the Lenin Peace Prize from the Soviet Union and has been nominated by the Quakers for the Nobel prize.

Born in 1924 in Trieste, Dolci gave up a promising career in architecture to work in a Christian commune for war orphans in Tuscany. He later moved to a part of Sicily that boasted the nation's highest crime rate and lowest literacy. In the following two decades, Dolci helped the villages build roads, dams, schools and cooperatives. In the process he fought Mafia control and created "strikes in reverse"—where villagers did public works without pay in order to dramatize the need for jobs. Dolci also fasted to secure state emergency funds to alleviate poverty in the region.

His current work now centers on the way conflict in family relationships sets the pattern for large-scale social violence. Dolci believes rage, doubt and insecurity must be dealt with in intimate relationships —before they become dangerous projectiles threatening the stability of international communities.

The Friends of Danilo Dolci, Inc., are active in many countries around the world. His translated books include *A New World in the Making, Sicilian Lives,* and a celebrated book of poetry, *Creature of Creatures.*

Education, Creativity, and Development

It has been astutely observed that apocalypse contains the sense of unveiling or revelation, as well as that of ending. Yet what should we think of this complex of intuitions and nightmares, of desires, dreams and catastrophic fears? I believe that, for a person who is aware, every day has its own apocalypse, every day unveils itself, every day goes into dust. I find one remark of Jung's very telling: each one of us can discover and defuse our most secret traumas in order to set in motion an alternative way of life.

To this end, I think it may be useful to explore the connection between education, creativity, and human development. Let us begin by looking at a current problem: all of us know that we are perfecting a monster known as the Trident. This submarine is two football fields long. It has 24 missiles, and each one of these missiles has 17 atomic bombs. Each one of these warheads is five times more powerful than the bomb that destroyed Hiroshima. Each one of us can do the simple multiplication, 24 times 17, and come up with 478. This is the number of cities that can be destroyed in less than five minutes, with incredible precision, with rocket thrusts that reach a distance of 6,000 miles. Naturally, this costs money. Two Tridents, we ought to know, cost the same as running the nation's entire public education system for a single year. So we have a choice.

And this is just one of our monsters! On this side of the globe, there are a thousand others just as dangerous. On the other side of the globe, there are the SS-4s, the SS-5s, up to the SS-18s and SS-20s. Everyone in the world should know these facts and ask,

"Can the world become a burnt-out ball of molten glass spinning through space?" On the other hand, we must recognize that the world could also become a creature alive with other creatures. It would give us great strength to have both these images, and they would be even more effective if we were to ask, "On whom does this depend?"

The answer to that, of course, is that it depends on each one of us. Each of us must ask, "How is it possible to bridge this enormous gap between the world as it is and the world as it might be?" I naturally have no prescription, no magic key. But I think we can begin by considering a few possible tools.

Let us take *education,* for example. We have this word constantly on our lips, yet experts know that our concepts of education are in their infancy. In truth, we know very little about education. Yet the strength of the expert is in knowing that he does not know.

In what sense, then, do I use the word *education*? The sense I give to that word is that of the midwife. Not that one person alone should become a midwife for the group. Each person can learn to be a midwife for others. In a process I call "popular self-analysis," people can slowly, deliberately come to an understanding of reality as it is—and reality as it *might* be.

I began my work in Sicily in a desperate situation where people were turning to banditry. The reason: they were hungry and there was no work. The state intervened with armed forces, and this was an enormous waste of blood, energy, and money. I began to work with a small group of collaborators, asking the people if they could come up with a lever to change the situation. We didn't preach; we asked questions. And little by little, small groups began to think and to ask themselves questions. Then, as the months went by, the idea for a possible solution came forth.

Someone said, "Here in the summer it doesn't rain, and the arid earth produces nothing. But during the winter, there are heavy rains and the water just runs off into the sea." Another timidly suggested, "Would it be possible to keep this water and use it in the summer?" These people had never heard of a dam, had never seen one before. The word they came up with for this was the word for the basin or washbowl in which they bathed their children. So we used this word and asked the people, "Do you want a basin to hold your water?" Some reacted, "That's too wonderful to be true!"

Others were inflamed with the idea. So we brought pressure on the government. We went to prison, we fasted, and eventually we were able to prevail upon the state to build a dam.

This is one example that illustrates how people can come up with a viable solution by looking within themselves. One dam more or less is not what matters here. What is important is recognizing the lever to change any situation, in any part of the world, that could transform the malcontents into a new source of power.

In the region I am talking about, no more than twenty people held in their hands all the political power. Most of the people were day laborers or small landholders who had no say in the way things were organized. As the dam was going up, we asked the people, "Do you want water that is expensive or cheap?" And they understood that, for the water to be cheap, it had to be not Mafia-controlled water, but democratic water. Slowly but surely they began to organize, and the dam itself became a new lever that brought about structural change in the society.

You can imagine that it takes longer to accomplish these things than it does to talk about them! And you can imagine how difficult it is for a population to believe that it is possible not only to change the land but to change the very structure of power and influence the decision-making process.

Let me give another, very different example. Imagine we have with us a scientist who is an expert in genetics. We ask him what goes on between the embryo and a pregnant woman, what is communicated between them? The scientist says we used to think it was a one-way transmission from the mother to the growing embryo, yet in the last few years we have realized that something passes from the embryo to the mother. This woman becomes completely different when she is pregnant; she becomes transfigured by adapting to creation. The scientist will say it's possible to speak about such adaptation, but we still don't know how it happens!

This question has enormous implications for the field of education. For example, will this adaptation continue between mother and child even after the child is born? Evidently it will. Yet at a certain moment the mother will have to leave the child—she cannot follow him to school. Should the person who takes the mother's place also be in the same relationship—that of adapting to creativity with the child?

I'll tell you some stories not just for the sake of telling them, but so that you can see what these stories echo in yourself.

First story. I am in a very rich and sleepy village in northern Italy. I have to be at work at six in the morning, and I want nothing more than a cup of coffee. As I walk down the street I see a woman dressed up in a fine fur coat. At the end of a leash, she has a little dog. The dog is very lively; it is sniffing all around. The woman—who is a literature teacher—keeps telling the dog to behave himself. "What are you looking at? There's nothing to look at!" she says. The dog's eyes are a little dazed. I think, "Right now it's 6 A.M. She has a dog on a leash. In two hours, she will have thirty kids on a leash."

Second story. I leave the sleepy, rich northern village and return to Partinico, Sicily, where I work. I drive to the square at noon and see a man doing something I can't quite figure out. Near his door, there is a jasmine plant so strong and thriving that it is almost a jasmine tree. I stop my car and ask, "What are you doing with these flowers? Making jasmine tea?" He turns around and looks at me with a radiant expression: "No, I am taking these flowers to put around the photographs of my mother and father." What a wonderful relationship this man has with the springs of his own life! And I, who am supposed to be a poet, thought he was making jasmine tea! As I am about to leave, he gives me all the flowers he has picked. "Here," he says. "Take them in your car. They smell beautiful." Dazed by this experience, I go home and explain what happened to my wife and children.

The next day, as I am passing through the square, I want to go and see this old man and tell him what I've learned from him. When I meet him, I explain, "Yesterday I was enchanted by our encounter." This man who has never read a book on education or science, who in fact has probably never read a single book, refused even for an instant to be placed on a superior level. When he saw how much I admired him, he immediately said, "What was it you told me yesterday—that you can make tea with the flowers, too?" Immediately I thought about the woman with the leash.

Second point: There's another word that is always on our lips. The word *creativity*. We should ask ourselves some questions about this, too. Breathing—is it a luxury or a necessity? To meditate—is that a luxury or a necessity? To imagine alternatives? To learn to dream? To distinguish illusions from reasonable desires?

Poetry—which is the extreme development of creativity—is this luxury or necessity? For one person—or for everyone? (When I say to make poetry, I mean with all kinds of materials, not just with words. Each of us knows you can make poetry with stones, with sounds, with movement.) We should also ask: "Why is it that people refuse creativity?"

I think the answer is that people do not wish to suffer. In fact, there are two kinds of pain in creativity. The first is like the pain of a woman giving birth. And the second is like the vertigo of the newborn infant as he comes into the world. We all know that one can give birth smiling. It depends on the awareness we have of what we are doing.

If somebody wants to get to Moscow, let's say, or to London, he is more likely to get there if he knows where he is going. If our imagination is able to produce specific desires, this gives us an element of strength. If the world is imagined as an earthly city, then there is more likelihood that it will come into being. If each one of us is capable of envisioning a world that is itself a creature filled with other living creatures, then this is more likely to come to pass.

In western Sicily, when the democratic irrigation system had begun to make the country fertile, we asked the people if they could think of another lever to change their situation even more profoundly. Slowly, after many meetings and discussions, they came up with the idea for an educational center. It was, above all, the women and children who produced this concept. So in the years that followed, we built a school. Last October, there was one particular child who had a lot of trouble and who constantly broke things. If his companions were building something with sticks, he would go by and knock it down. He brought all of his difficulties with him from his family environment.

Each morning the teacher would ask the children what they wanted to do. Then the teacher would express his or her idea, and together they would work out a plan for the day's work. This boy refused to take part in the discussion, until one day somebody made a proposal that intrigued him. One of the children said, "It's a nice day. Let's go out and crush olives and prepare them for eating later in the week." Perhaps it was the idea of crushing something, or perhaps it was just the idea of going outside in the open air, but for the first time, the boy reacted and said, "Yes, let's do that!"

So the children started picking the ripest, biggest olives and began crushing them. This kid had found a rock with a crack in it. He lined up all the olives in this crack and was the best at crushing them. All the other children gathered around him to see how quick he was. Now, feeling that he was admired and was the center of attention, he became the teacher, explaining to the other kids how he was doing this. This was a beginning: little by little, in the following weeks, the boy was brought back into the group. (Of course, there were still problems. You know that nothing happens as in fairy tales.)

Second story. A doctor named Basaglia arrived in a mental asylum in Trieste. What he found was basically a prison. He noticed that some of the people there simply did not speak to each other anymore. Instead, some of them went out and spoke to an old horse in the courtyard. They told their secrets to the horse, but some time later the horse died, so the patients had a meeting. You can imagine their sadness. One of the patients asked, "What are we going to do now?" Another replied, "Let's make a horse." "How?" The patient pulled a piece of chalk out of his pocket and drew a marvelous horse on the wall. He was also an expert in papier-mâché sculpting, and so he got them all together and they made a horse out of paper. The whole asylum worked to produce an incredible blue horse. A month later, when it was finished, one patient said, "We have to have a party!" Said another, "We should take the horse into the main square so that everyone can see it."

One objected: "That's a great idea, but how do we get the horse out the door?" Another patient replied, "Don't worry—we'll move the beams near the door."

The doctor listened, let them do as they wanted, and got some wheels ready for the next day. Then a small miracle occurred: they pulled the horse into the public square and the people, amazed at the sight of this enormous blue horse, asked, "What is this?" The patients who hadn't spoken for years began explaining what it was!

Another word that is always on our lips is *development.* If we pay attention to the way people use this word, we see that there is a great deal of confusion about it. Most people use the words *creativity* and *development* as if they were synonymous. To develop is to augment, to enlarge, to amplify, to lengthen. But when we see a piece of spaghetti coming out of a spaghetti machine, that is not development! This example that makes you laugh is really at the root of one of the largest misunderstandings of our time.

The definition of *development* is interesting: development is "a coordination of processes, designed to produce an organized heterogeneity." But who is responsible for this definition? A sociologist or a politician? A biologist?

Let me tell you one final story. I was teaching at a university in southern Italy, and in order to get to know the students better I went to visit a small village at the top of a hill. I left my car and wandered around looking at the houses. It was a magnificent view: the yards were very tidy, planted with geraniums and other flowers. The smell of freshly-baked bread was in the air. As it began to rain, I walked back toward my car. A couple of boys waved at me and asked me to give them a ride down the hill. One of them asked with the frankness that young people have, "What did you come here for?" I said I came to see the village because I had never been there before. They asked me, "What did you think of it?" Without thinking very much I said, "It's a beautiful place, but it looks pretty poor." One of them replied—and not in an aggressive way, "Poor in what sense?" I thought to myself, when I heard this, "If this is not culture, then what is?"

All of us know that small children are not particularly coordinated. When they are infants, their hands are not coordinated with their minds. The question I sometimes ask myself is whether or not the earth is an infant that is still basically uncoordinated and still not able to recognize itself, as children are unable to recognize themselves. Scientists refer to the biosphere, that is, the sphere of life. If we think of a missile that is about to take off, we should feel it as a wound that is about to tear into our flesh. If we are able to think in these terms, each day will signify more profoundly its revelation.

(Interpreted by Anthony Oldcorn)

JAMES HILLMAN

James Hillman is known internationally as the leading voice of renewal in the psychoanalytic tradition of C. G. Jung. A Founding Fellow of the Dallas Institute of Humanities and Culture, Dr. Hillman is a diplomate analyst of the Jung Institute in Zürich where he also served as Director of Studies from 1959–1969. Currently, he is the editor and publisher of Spring Publications which specializes in imaginal psychology.

Of his many publications, *Re-Visioning Psychology* and *The Dream and the Underworld* have marked major breakthroughs in the study of the imagination. His most recent works are *Freud's Own Cookbook* (with Charles Boer) and *Anima: An Anatomy of a Personified Notion*.

Wars, Arms, Rams, Mars
On the Love of War

You will recall, if you saw the film *Patton,* the scene in which the American General, who commanded the Third Army in the 1944–45 drive across France into Germany, walks the field after a battle: churned earth, burnt tanks, dead men. The General takes up a dying officer, kisses him, surveys the havoc, and says: "I love it. God help me I do love it so. I love it more than my life."

This scene gives focus to my theme—the love of war, the love in war and for war that is more than 'my' life, a love that calls up a God, that is helped by a God and on a battlefield, a devastated piece of earth that is made sacred by that devastation.

I believe we can never speak sensibly of peace or disarmament unless we enter into this love of war. Unless we enter into the martial state of soul, we cannot comprehend its pull. This special state must be ritualistically entered. We must be 'inducted,' and war must be 'declared'—as one is declared insane, declared married or bankrupt. So we shall try now to 'go to war' and this because it is a principle of psychological method that any phenomenon to be understood must be empathically imagined. To know war we must enter its love. No psychic phenomenon can be truly dislodged from its fixity unless we first move the imagination into its heart.

War is a psychological task, which Freud recognized and addressed in several papers. It is especially a psychological task because philosophy and theology have failed its over-riding importance. War has been set aside as history, where it then becomes a sub-chapter called military history. Or, war has been placed outside the mainstream of thought into think-tanks. So we need to lift this general repression, attempting to bring to war an imagination that respects its primordial significance.

My method of heading right in, of penetrating rather than circumambulating or reflecting, is itself martial. So we shall be invoking the God of the topic by this approach to the topic.

During the 5,600 years of written history, there have been at least 14,600 recorded wars. Two or three wars each year of human history. Since Edward Creasy's *Fifteen Decisive Battles* (1851), we have been taught that the turning points of Western civilization occur in battles such as Salamis and Marathon, Carthage, Tours, Lepanto, Constantinople, Waterloo, Midway, Stalingrad. . . . The ultimate determination of historical fate, we have been taught, depends upon battle, whose outcome in turn depends upon an invisible genius in a leader or hero through whom a transcendent spirit is manifested. The battle and its personified epitome become salvational representations in secular history. The statues in our parks, the names of our grand avenues, and the holidays we celebrate commemorate the salvational aspect of battle.

Neglected in Creasy's decisive battles are the thousands of indecisive ones, fought with equal heroism, yet which ended inconclusively or yielded no victory for the ultimate victor of the war; nor did these battles produce commemorative epic, statue or celebration. Unsung heroes; died in vain; lost cause. The ferocity of battle may have little to do with its outcome, the outcome little to do with the outcome of the war. Verdun in the Great War of 1914–18 is such an example: a million casualties and nothing decisive. The significance of a battle is not given by the war, but by the battle itself.

Besides the actual battles and their monuments, the monumental epics that lie in the roots of our Western languages are to a large proportion 'war books': the *Mahabarata* and its *Bhagavad Gita,* the *Iliad,* the *Aenead,* the Celtic *Lebor Gabala,* and the Norse *Edda.* Our Bible is a long account of battles, of wars and captains of wars. Jahweh presents himself in the speeches of a War God, and his prophets and kings are his warriors.[1] Even the New Testament is so arranged that its final culminating chapter, Revelation, functions as its recapitulative coda in which the Great Armageddon of the Apocalypse is its crisis.

In our most elevated works of thought—Hindu and Platonic philosophy—a warrior class is imagined as necessary to the well-being of humankind. This class finds its counterpart within human nature, in the heart, as virtues of courage, nobility, honor, loyalty, steadfastness of principle, comradely love, so that war is given location not only in a class of persons but in a level of human personality organically necessary to the justice of the whole.

Have I carried my first point that battles and the martial are not merely irrational relapses into archaic pre-civilization? The martial cannot be derived merely from the territorial imperative of our animal inheritance: "this is my realm, my feeding and breeding space; get out or I'll kill you." Nor do wars arise simply from industrial capitalism and its economic distress, the mystiques of tribes and nationalism, the just preservation of a state, masculine machoism, sociological indoctrinations or psychological paranoia and aggression. (Paranoia and aggression, if explanatory principles, themselves require explanations.) No, wars are not only man-made; they bear witness also to something essentially human that transcends the human, invoking powers more than the human can fully grasp. Not only do Gods battle among themselves and against other foreign Gods, they sanctify human wars, and they participate in those wars by divine intervention, as when soldiers hear divine voices and see divine visions in the midst of battle.

Because of this transcendent infiltration, wars are so difficult to control and understand. What takes place in battle is always to some degree mysterious, and therefore unpredictable, never altogether in human hands. Wars "break out." Once commanders sought signs in the heavens, from birds. Today, we fantasize the origin of war in a computer accident. *Fortuna*—despite meticulous battle plans and rehearsals, the battle experience is a melee of surprises.

We therefore require an account of war that allows for its transcendent moment, an account that roots itself in *archai*—the Greek word for "first principle"—*arché,* not merely as archaic, a term of historical explanation, but as archetypal, evoking the trans-historical background, that divine epiphanic moment in war.[2]

This archetypal approach holds that ever-recurring, ubiquitous, highly ritualized and passionate events are governed by fundamental psychic patterning factors. These factors are given with the world as modes of its psychological nature, much as patterns of atomic behavior are given with the physical nature of the world and patterns of instinctual behavior are given with the world's biological nature.

I want now for us to enter more closely into the epiphany of this archetypal principle, this God, Mars. Here is a reading from Ernst Junger's diary, recording the start of the last German offensive in 1918:

> The great moment had come. The curtain of fire lifted from the front trenches. We stood up—we moved in step, irresistibly toward the enemy lines. I was boiling with a mad rage, which had taken hold of me and all others in an incomprehensible fashion. The overwhelming wish to kill gave wings to my feet. The monstrous desire for annihilation, which hovered over the battlefield, thickened the brains of the men in a red fog. We called each other in sobs and stammered disconnected sentences. A neutral observer might perhaps have believed we were seized by an excess of happiness.[3]

A scholar of Japanese culture, Donald Keene, has collected *tanka* and hundreds of other writings expressing the feelings of major Japanese authors (including liberals, leftists and Christians) during the 1941–45 war. I shall quote only passages referring to Pearl Harbor. Nagayo Yoshio, author of *The Bronze Christ,* on hearing of the declaration of war with the United States, wrote: "I never thought that in this lifetime I should ever know such a happy, thrilling, auspicious experience." The novelist and critic Ito Sei on the same occasion said: "I felt as if in one stroke I had become a new man, from the depths of my being." Honda Akira, scholar of English literature, wrote: "I have felt the sense of a clearing. Now the word 'holy war' is obvious . . . a new courage has welled up and everything has become easier to do."

Glenn Gray, in his book *The Warriors*—the most sensitive account of war experience that I know—writes:

> . . . veterans who are honest with themselves will admit the ex-

perience in battle has been a high point in their lives. Despite the horror, the weariness, the grime, and the hatred, participation with others in the chances of battle had its unforgettable side. For anyone who has not experienced it himself, the feeling is hard to comprehend and for the participant hard to explain to anyone else—that curious combination of earnestness and lightheartedness so often noted of men in battle.[4]

These positive experiences are puzzling. It is the positive experience that we must reckon with because the savagery and confusion, the exhaustion and desertion correspond with what is objectively taking place. Those responses do not need explanations. But how mystifying the lightheartedness in killing, the joy of going into battle, and that infantrymen with bayonets fixed, snipers in ambush, torpedo men in destroyers report no particular hatred, little heroic ambition, unconcern for victory, or even passion for their cause for which they stand exposed and may even volunteer to die. Instead, they sometimes report altered states of perception, intensified vitality, a new awareness of the earth's beauty and nearness of divinity—their little plot, their meager, grimy life suddenly transcendently sweet. "It is well that war is so terrible," said Robert E. Lee, "we would grow too fond of it."

And, beyond all else is the group-bonding to the platoon, the crew, a buddy.[5] Love in war. Thomas Aquinas notes that comrades in arms display a specific form of friendship. This battle-love is complex, gentle, altruistic and fierce. It cannot be reduced merely to modern psychologisms: boosting masculinity with macho codes of honor, peer-pressure that successfully represses cowardice, the discovery and release under the duress of battle of repressed homosexual emotion. Moreover, so strong and so transcending the aims of war itself is this love that a soldier, in fidelity to his buddies, may more easily shoot down his own officer than an enemy in the opposite trench.

To illustrate this love in war, I shall condense from S. L. A. Marshall an incident from his account of the desperate American retreat from the Yalu after the failed invasion of North Korea.[6] There was a tight ravine under enemy fire through which funnel the only escape route lay. "From end to end this sanctuary was already filled with bodies, the living and the dead, wounded men who could no longer move, the exhausted . . . the able-bodied driven to earth by fire. It was a sump pit of all who had become detached from their vehicles and abandoned to each other . . . 200 men in the ditch so that their bodies overlapped. Americans, Turks, ROK's. . . . Yet there was cooperative motion and human response. Men who were still partly mobile crawled forward along the chain of bodies. . . . As they moved, those who were down and hurt cried: 'Water! Water!' . . . Long since, nearly all canteens were dry. But the able-bodied checked long enough to do what bandaging they could . . . some stripped to the waist in the bitter cold and tore up their undershirts for dressings. Others stopped their crawl long enough to give their last drop of water . . . the wounded who were bound to the ditch tried to assist the able-bodied seeking to get out. Witnesses saw more of the decency of men than ever had been expected."

Love and war have traditionally been coupled in the figures of Venus and Mars, Aphrodite and Ares. This usual allegory is expressed in usual slogans—make love not war, all's fair in love and war—and in usual oscillating behaviors—rest, recreation and rehabilitation in the whorehouse behind the lines, then return to the all-male barracks. Instead of these couplings which actually separate Mars and Venus into alternatives, there is a Venusian experience within Mars itself. It occurs in the sensate love of life in the midst of battle, in the care for concrete details built into all martial regulations, in the sprucing, prancing and dandying of the cavaliers (now called "boys") on leave. Are they sons of Mars or of Venus?

In fact, we need to look again at the aesthetic aspect of Mars. Also there a love lies hidden. From the civilian sidelines, military rites and rhetoric seem kitsch and pomposity. But look instead at this language, these procedures as the sensitization by ritual of the physical imagination. Consider how many different kinds of blades, edges, points, metals and temperings are fashioned on the variety of knives, swords, spears, sabers, battle-axes, rapiers, daggers, lances, pikes, halberds that have been lovingly honed with the idea for killing. Look at the rewards for killing: Iron Cross, Victoria Cross, Medal of Honor, Croix de Guerre; the accoutrements: bamboo baton, swagger stick, epaulets, decorated sleeves, ivory-handled pistols. The music: reveille and taps, drums and pipes, fifes and drums, trumpets, bugles, the marching songs and marching bands, brass, braid, stripes. The military tailors: Wellington boots, Eisenhower jackets, Sam Brown belts, green berets, red coats, "whites."[7] Forms, ranks, promotions. Flags, banners, trooping to the colors. The military mess—its postures, toasts. The manners: salutes, drills, commands. Martial rituals of the feet—turns, steps, paces, warriors' dances. Of the eyes—eyes front! Of the hands, the neck, the voice, ramrod backbone, abdomen—"Suck in that gut, soldier." The names: Hussars, Dragoons, Rangers, Lancers, Coldstream Guards, and nicknames: bluejacket, leatherneck, doughboy. The great walls and bastions of severe beauty built by Brunelleschi, da Vinci, Michelangelo, Buontalenti. The decorated horse, notches in the rifle stock, the painted emblems on metal equipment, letters from the front, poems. Spit and polish and pent emotion. Neatsfoot oil, gunsmith, swordsmith; the Shield of Achilles on which is engraved the whole world.

Our American consciousness has extreme difficulty with Mars.[8] Our founding documents and legends portray the inherent nonmartial bias of our civilian democracy. You can see this in the second, third and fourth constitutional amendments which severely restrict military power in the civilian domain. You can see this in the stories of the Massachusetts Minutemen versus European mercenaries and redcoats, and in the Green Mountain boys and the soldiers of the Swamp Fox—civilians all. And you can see it in the casual, individualistic Texans at San Jacinto versus the Mexican officers trained in the European mold.

Compared with our background in Europe, Americans are idealistic: war has no place. It should not be. War is not glorious, triumphal, creative as to a warrior class in Europe from Rome and the Normans through the Crusades even to the Battle of Britain. We may be a violent people but not a warlike people—and our hatred of war makes us use violence against even war itself. Wanting to put a stop to it was a major cause of the Los Alamos project and Truman's decision to bomb Hiroshima *and* Nagasaki, a bomb to "save lives," a bomb to end bombs, like the idea of a war to end all wars. "The object of war," it says on General Sherman's statue in Washington, "is a more perfect peace." Our so-called doublespeak about armaments as "peacekeepers" reflects truly how we think. War is bad, exterminate war and keep peace violently:

punitive expeditions, pre-emptive strikes, send in the Marines. More fire-power means surer peace. We enact the blind God's blindness (Mars *Caecus,* as the Romans called him, and Mars *insanus, furibundus, omnipotens*), like General Grant in the Wilderness, like the bombing of Dresden, overkill as a way to end war.

Gun control is a further case in point. It raises profound perplexities in a civilian society. The right to bear arms is constitutional, and our nation and its territorial history (for better or for worse) have depended on a citizen-militia's familiarity with weapons. But that was when the rifle and the Bible (together with wife and dog) went alone into the wilderness. The gun was backed by a God; when it stood in the corner of the household, pointing upward like the Roman spear that *was* Mars, the remembrance of the God was there, and the awe and even some ceremony. With the neglect of Mars, we are left only the ego and the guns that we try to control with civilian secular laws.

If in the arms is the God, then arms control requires at least partly, if not ultimately, a religious approach. The statement by the Catholic Bishops is a harbinger of that recognition. We worry about nuclear accident, but what we call "accident" is the autonomy of the inhuman. Arms, as instruments of death, are sacred objects that remind mortals that we are not *athnetos,* immortal. The fact that arms control negotiations take on more and more ritualistic postures rather than negotiating positions also indicates the transcendent power of the arms over those who would bring them under control. Military expenditures of course "overrun," and handguns "get out of hand." I do not believe arms control can come about until the essential nature of arms is first recognized.

Our immigrant dream of escape from conscription into the deadly games of Mars on the European battlefields cannot fit Mars into the American utopia. Hence that paradox for Americans of a peacetime draft and the violence that conscription can occasion. This clash of archetypal perspectives—civil and military—appears sharply in Sicily in 1943 when General Patton slapped two conscripted soldiers who were in the hospital for anxiety states.[9] To the appalled General (a son of Mars), they were malingerers, cowards without love for their fellows. To the appalled American nation of civilians, Patton was the coward, slapping the defenseless sick, without love of his fellows.

By the way, our customary language betrays a bias in favor of the civil—simply by calling it civil. Were we speaking from the military perspective, "civil" would be called "merchant," for these were the traditional class terms in many societies, including India and Japan, and in the Platonic division where the merchants were lower than the warriors (*Phaedrus* 248d) who were not permitted property (*Republic* IV). Traditionally, the warrior class favors the son; the merchant class, the daughter. By slapping his soldiers, Patton was treating them as sons; the civilian (i.e., merchant) reaction experiences them as mistreated daughters.

Although the office of President does combine civil and military, head-of-state and commander-in-chief, and though that office has been held by notable generals—Washington, Jackson, Grant and Eisenhower—and men with military careers, it has been the habit in recent years for the presidency to founder upon this double role: I think of Truman and Korea, Kennedy and the Bay of Pigs, Johnson and Vietnam, Carter and Iran, and now perhaps Reagan and Central America. Unlike the Roman Republic where Jupiter and Mars could rule together, our republic pretends to have no God of War, not even a department of war. This repression of Mars rather than ritualization of Mars leaves us exposed to the return of the repressed, as rude eruptive violence, as anxiety about armaments and military expenditures, as rigid reaction formations disguised as peace negotiations, and as paranoid defenses against delusional enemies.

So far I have been stressing the distinction between the military and civil imaginations. I have considered each to be moved by its own archetypal power, powers that do not easily accommodate in a secular monotheistic consciousness, because that consciousness identifies with a single point of view, forcing others into opponents. Oppositional thinking and true believing are makers of this consciousness.

Now, let me make a second distinction between the military and nuclear imaginations: the martial is not necessarily nuclear nor is the nuclear necessarily martial. The civilian rejection of Mars, however, has so pushed the martial over into the nuclear that we can't think of war without thinking of nuclear war. Mr. Reagan, in fact, calls war "the unthinkable," a mystic's notion of a God beyond thought, beyond image. War is not unthinkable, and not to think it, not to imagine it, only favors the mystical appeal of apocalyptic nuclearism. Remember Hannah Arendt's call to thinking? Not to think, not to imagine is the behavior of Eichmann, said Hannah Arendt. So let us go on thinking all we can about Mars, now in distinction with the nuclear.

Mars in the Roman Republic, where he was most developed as a distinct figure, was placed in a Champs du Mars, a field, a terrain. He was so earthbound that many scholars trace the origins of the Mars cult to agriculture. This helps my point: Mars did not belong to the city. Not until Julius Caesar and caesarism were troops allowed in the city. The focus of martial activity has usually been less the conquest of cities than of terrain and the destruction of armies occupying terrain. Even the naval war in the Pacific (1941–45) followed this classical intention of gaining area.

The martial commander must sense the lay of the land. He is a geographer. The horse (an animal of Mars) was so essential for martial peoples because horses could realize the strategy of winning terrain. Martial strategy is archetypally geo-political.

The nuclear imagination, in contrast, calculates in terms of cities, and its destructive fantasies necessarily include civilians. The city (and thus the civilization, whether taken out by ICBMs or kept as intact prizes by the neutron weapon) is the main focus of the nuclear imagination. The land between Kiev and Pittsburgh (hence Europe) is relatively irrelevant.

A second contrast between the martial and the nuclear: Mars moves in close, hand-to-hand, Mars *propior* and *propinquus*. Bellona is a fury, the blood-dimmed tide, the red fog of intense immediacy. No distance. Acquired skills become instantaneous as in the martial arts. The nuclear imagination, in contrast, invents at ever greater distance—intercontinental, the bottom of the sea, outer space. Because of the time delay caused by distance, the computer becomes *the* essential nuclear weapon. The computer is the only way to regain the instantaneity given archetypally with Mars. The computer controls nuclear weapons, is their governor. Whereas the martial is contained less by fail-safe devices and rational computation than by military ritual of disciplined hierarchy, practiced skill, repetition, code, and inspection. And by the concrete obstacles of geography: commissary trains, hedgerows, bad weather, *impedimenta*.

Our civilian republic has not become fully conscious of the distinction I am laboring. The civilian soldier rebels against military rituals as senseless. He does not grasp that they serve to contain the God of War and so must be obeyed—as Patton insisted—religiously, as if the military were a religious order.

So, too, our civilian republic is not enough aware of the distinction between military and nuclear, thereby entrusting the control of nuclear explosions to the military in the person of General Grove. Considering the volatile commixture of the God of War with the spiritual, apocalyptic appeal of nuclearism, it is miraculous that we have had only test blasts.

A further difference between martial and nuclear is in their visions of transcendence. They show two elemental imaginations of fire: war and the fire of earth; apocalypse and the fire of ether or air. And two different animals: the ram of territory and head-on collision; the eagle of piercing surprise and the uplifting rapture of nuclearism.

The nuclear imagination, further, is without ancestry. Nothing to look back on and draw upon. History provides no precedents. There is a broken connection, to use Lifton's phrase, between sudden, hideous and collective extinction and deaths modeled by the ancestors. The martial imagination is steeped in memorials. Past battles and military biographies are the ongoing texts. We tramp the battlefields, ponder the cemeteries. There are Swiss depictions of battles, for instance, showing skeletons in the ranks: here are the ancestors fighting in our midst.

The rhetoric of Mars in war-journals, poems and recollections speaks of attachment to specific earthly places, comrades, things. The transcendent is in the concrete particular. Hemingway writes that, after World War I, "abstract words such as glory, honor, courage . . . were obscene beside the concrete names of villages, the numbers of roads, the names of rivers, the regiments and dates." How rare for anyone to know the date of Alamogordo (or even where it is), the date of Hiroshima, of the first hydrogen bomb explosion, or the names of people or places or units engaged. Gone in abstraction. Glenn Gray writes: "Any fighting unit must have a limited and specific objective. A physical goal—a piece of earth to defend, a machine gun nest to destroy, a strong point to annihilate—more likely evokes a sense of comradeship."[10]

Martial psychology turns events into images: physical, bound-ed, named. Hurtgen Forest, Vimy Ridge, Iwo Jima. A beach, a bridge, a railroad crossing: battle places become iconic and sacred, physical images claiming the utmost human love, worth more than my life.

Quite different is the transcendent experience of the nuclear fireball. The emotion is stupefaction at destruction itself rather than a heightened regard for the destroyed. Nuclear devastation is not merely a deafening cannonade or fire-bombing carried to a further degree. It is different in kind; archetypally different. It evokes the apocalyptic transformation of the world into fire, earth ascending in a pillar of cloud, an epiphanic fire revealing the inmost spirit of all things, as in the Buddha's fire sermon:

> All things, O priests, are on fire . . . the mind is on fire, ideas are on fire . . . mind consciousness is on fire.

Or like that passage from the *Bhagavad Gita* which came to Oppenheimer when he saw the atomic blast:

> If the radiance of a thousand suns
> Were burst at once into the sky
> That would be like the splendour of the Mighty One.

The nuclear imagination leaves the human behind for the worst sin of all: fascination by the spirit. *Superbia.* The soul goes up in fire. If the epiphany in battle unveils love of this place and that man and values more than my life, yet bound with this world, and its life, the nuclear epiphany unveils the apocalyptic God, a God of extinction, the God-is-dead God, an epiphany of Nihilism.

Apocalypse is not necessary to war. Let me make this very clear: apocalypse is not part of the myths of Mars. Mars asks for battle, not wipeout, not even victory. (*Nike* belongs to Athene, not Ares.) Patton supposedly said: "I like making things happen. That's my share in Deity." Apocalypse is inherent, not in the Martial deity, but in the Christian deity. Fascination with a transcendent Christ may be more the threat to the Christian civilization than the War God himself. Are not civilizations saved by their Gods also led to destruction by those same, their own, Gods?

There is one more distinction, one that may be of the most therapeutic significance. If nuclearism produces "psychic numbing," stupefaction, stupidity, Mars works precisely to the contrary. He intensifies the senses and heightens fellow-feeling in action, that energized vivification the Romans called "Mars *Nerio*" and "Mars *Moles*," molar, massive, making things happen. Mobilization. Mars gives answer to the hopelessness and drifting powerlessness we feel in the face of nuclear weapons by awakening fear, Phobos, his Greek companion or son, and rage, *ira,* wrath. Mars is the instigator, the primordial activist. To put the contrast in eschatological terms, Mars is the God of Beginnings, the sign of the Ram. March is his month, and April, Mars *Apertus,* opening, making things happen. Apocalypse may lift veils, but it closes down into the truly final solution, after which there is no re-opening, no *recorso.* Broken the wheel.

I seem to have been making a case for the lesser of two evils, and to have so favored Mars that you may have heard me as a war-monger. But this would be to hear me only literally. Rather than warmonger, see me as ram-monger, Mars-lover. Take my talk as a devotional ritual of imagination to constellate his awakening power. In this way we may call him up and yet deliteralize him at the same time.

It was an ancient custom and is still a modern psychological technique to turn for aid to the very same principle that causes an affliction. The cure of the Mars we fear is the God himself. One must approximate his affects in order to differentiate them. "The Homeric Hymn to Mars" (Ares), in Charles Boer's translation, makes this clear:

> Hear me
> helper of mankind,
> beam down from up there
> your gentle light
> on our lives
> and your martial power
> so that I can shake off
> cruel cowardice
> from my head
> and diminish that deceptive rush

of my spirit, and restrain
that shrill voice in my heart
that provokes me
to enter the chilling din of battle.
You, happy God
give me courage
to linger in the safe laws of peace
and thus escape
from battles with enemies
and the fate of violent death.[11]

It seems that the more we can love Mars, as in this hymn, the more we can discriminate (to use its words): the deceptive rush of the spirit, the shrill voice that provokes into battle, and at the same time shakes off cruel cowardice from my head.

This imaginative devotion to Mars provides a mode of deliteralizing beyond interpretation of the meaning of the God, beyond a mental act of seeing-through. Here, by deliteralizing I mean: to be fundamentally penetrated by an archetypal power, to participate in its style of love so that its compulsion gives way to its imagination, its angelic, message-giving intelligence. Then the God is experienced in the event as its image, the event no longer requiring my psychologizing for the image to be revealed.

Just this is my aim now, right now as I am speaking: not to explore war or apocalypse in the service of prevention, but to experience war and apocalypse so that their imaginations become fully realized, real. *We* cannot prevent; only images can help us; only images provide *providentia,* protection, prevention. That has always been the function of images: the magic of sacred protection.

We do not know much nowadays about imagining divinities. We have lost the angelic imagination and its angelic protection. It has fallen from all curricula—theological, philosophical, aesthetic. That loss may be more of a danger than either war or apocalypse because that loss results in literalism, the cause of both. As Lifton says, "The task now is to imagine the real." However, like so much of our imagination of the archetypal themes in human nature, the wars we now imagine are severely limited by modern positivistic consciousness. We imagine wars utterly without soul or spirit or

Gods, just as we imagine biological and psychological life, social intercourse and politics, the organization of nature—all without soul, spirit or Gods. Things without images.

Wars show this decline of ritual and increase of positivism, beginning with Napoleon and the War between the States (1861–65). The Great War of 1914–18 was stubborn, massive, unimaginative; the dark Satanic mill relocated in Flanders, sixty thousand British casualties in one single day on the Somme, and the same battle repeated and repeated like a positivist experiment or a positivist logical argument. The repetition of senselessness. Our wars become senseless when they have no myths. Guadalcanal, Inchon, My Lai: battles, casualties, graves (at best); statistics of firepower and body-count—but no myths. The reign of quantity, utterly literal.

Lacking a mythical perspective that pays homage to the God in war, we run the dangers of both war 'breaking out' and 'loving war too much'—and a third one: not being able to bring a war to a proper close. The Allies' demand for "unconditional surrender" only prolonged the Second World War, giving "justification" for the atomic bomb. Polybius and Talleyrand knew better: masters of war know how and where and when to ease out the God's fury. The very idea of an unconditional surrender evokes the blind rage of Mars *caecus, insanus,* the last-ditch suicidal effort. Surrender requires ritual, a *rite de sortie* that honors the God and allows his warriors to separate themselves from his dominion.

My thoughts have been intended to regain the mythical perspective. My thoughts have not been aimed at finding another literal answer to either war or nuclearism. We each know the literal answer: freeze, defuse, dismantle, disarm. Disarm the positivism but rearm the God; return arms and their control to the mythical realities that are their ultimate governances. Above all: wake up. To wake up, we need Mars, the God of Awakenings. Allow him to instigate our consciousness so that we may "escape the fate of violent death" and live the martial peace of activism.

A Frenchwoman after the Second World War tells Glenn Gray: "Anything is better than to have nothing at all happen day after day. You know I do not love war or want it to return. But at least it made me feel alive, as I have not felt before or since."[12]

Imagine! Is she not saying that war results not from the absence of the God but from his presence? For we long for purposeful action, hand-to-hand engagements, life lived in terms of death, seriousness and lightheartedness together, a clearing. The Frenchwoman's "nothing at all . . . day after day" is the nihilism of the nuclear age. Nuclear doom occurs not only in the literal future out there when the bomb goes off. Doom is already there in our numbed skulls, day-after-day, nothing-at-all. Mars can awaken us out of this nihilism, and its realization in an Apocalypse, with his *phobos,* fear. It may be our most precious emotion. We have everything to fear, except fear itself.

I have tied our numbing with a blocked imagination and the blocked imagination with the repression of Mars and his kind of love. But fifty minutes, as we know from psychotherapy, isn't going to lift very much repression. I hope, however, that I have been able to evoke enough of Mars for you to feel him stir in your anger and your fear, and in the outward extension of imagination that will probe such questions as:

How lay out the proper field of action for Mars? In what ways can martial love of killing and dying and martial fellowship serve a civilian society? How can we break apart the fusion of the martial and the nuclear? What modes are there for moving the martial away from direct violence toward indirect ritual? Can we bring the questions themselves into the post-modern consciousness of imaginal psychology, deconstruction and catastrophe theory? Can we deconstruct the positivism and literalism—epitomized by the ridiculous *counting* of warheads—that inform current policies before those policies literally and positively deconstruct our life, our history and our world?

Let us invoke Mars. At least once before in our century he pointed the way. During the years he reigned—1914–1918—he destroyed the nineteenth-century mind and brought forth modern consciousness. Could a turn to him now do something similar?

Yet Mars wants more than reflection. The ram does not pull back to consider, and iron takes no polish in which it can see itself. Mars demands penetration toward essence, pushing forward ever further into the tangle of danger, and danger now lies in the unthought thicket of our numbed minds. Swords must be *beaten* into plowshares, hammered, twisted, wrought.

Strangely enough, I think this deconstruction is already going on, so banally that we miss it. Is the translation of war from physical battlefield to television screen and space fiction, this translation of literal war into media, mediated war, and the fantasy language of wargames, staging areas, theaters of war and theater commanders, worstcase scenarios, rehearsals, and the Commander-in-Chief, an actor—is all this possibly pointing to a new mode of ritualizing war by imagining it?

If so, then the television war of Vietnam was not lost. The victims died not only for their cause (if there was one) or their country (if it cared). They were rather the sacrificial actors in a ritual that may deconstruct war wholly into an imaginal operation. Carl Sandburg's phrase, "Someday they'll give a war and no one will come," may have already begun. No one need come because the services for Mars are performed nightly at home on the tube. In a media society, will not capitalist war-profiteering shift its base from a military-industrial complex to a military-communications/information complex, the full symbolization of war?

If war could be contained in imagination, why not as well the nuclear bomb? A translation of the bomb into imagination keeps it safe from both military Martialism and civilian Christianism. The first would welcome it for an arm, the second for an Apocalypse. Imagination seems anyway to be the only safe place to keep the bomb: there is no literal positive place on earth where it can be held, as we cannot locate our MX missiles anywhere except as images on a drawing board or dump the wastes from manufacturing them anywhere safe.

However—to hold the bomb as image in the mind requires an extraordinary extension, and extraordinary daring, in our imagining powers, a revolution of imagination itself, enthroning it as the main, the greatest reality, because the bomb, which imagination shall contain, is the most powerful image of our age. Brighter than a thousand suns, it is our omnipotent God-term (as Wolfgang Giegerich has expounded), our mystery that requires constant imaginative propitiation. The translation of bomb into the imagination is a transubstantiation of God to *imago dei,* deliteralizing the ultimate God term from positivism to negative theology, a God that is all images. And, no more than any other God term can it be controlled by reason or taken fully literally without hideous consequences. The task of nuclear psychology is a ritual-like devotion to the bomb as image, never letting it slip from its pillar of cloud in the heaven of imagination to rain ruin on the cities of the plain.

The Damocles sword of nuclear catastrophe that hangs upon our minds is already producing utterly new patterns of thought about catastrophe itself, a new theology, a new science, a new psychology, not only burdening the mind with doom but forcing it into post-modern consciousness, displacing, deconstructing and trashing every fixed surety. Trashing is the symptom, and it indicates a psychic necessity of this age. To trash the end of the century of its coagulated notions calls for the disciplined ruthlessness and courage of Mars. Deconstructing the blocked mind, opening the way in faith with our rage and fear, stimulating the anaesthetized senses: this is psychic activism of the most intense sort.

Then—rather than obliterate the future with a bomb, we would deconstruct our notion of 'future,' take apart Western Futurism, that safe repository of our noble visions. Care, foresight, renewal, the Kingdom—these have been postponed forever into the future. Rather than blast the material earth with a bomb, we would deconstruct our entombment in materialism with its justification and salvation by economics. We would bomb the bottom line back to the stone age to find again values that are sensate and alive. Rather than bring time to a close with a bomb, we would deconstruct the positivistic imagination of time that has separated it from eternity.

In other words: explode the notions; let them go up in a spirited fire. Explode worldliness, not this world; explode final judgments; explode salvation and redemption and the comings and goings of Messiahs—is not the continual presence of here and now enough for you? Put hope back into the jar of evils and let go your addiction to hopeful fixes. Explode endings and fresh starts and the wish to be born again out of continuity. Release continuity from history: remember the animals and the archaic peoples who have continuity without history. (Must the animals and the archaic peoples go up in flames because of our sacred writ?) Then timelessness could go right on being revealed without Revelation, the veils of literalism pierced by intelligence, parting and falling to the mind that imagines and so welcomes the veiling. No sudden rendering, no apocalyptic ending; timelessness as the ongoing, the extraordinarily loving, lovable and terrifying continuity of life.

1. Cf. Millard C. Lind, *Yahweh Is a Warrior* (Scottdale, Pa.: Herald Press, 1980).

2. Compare Patton (*The Secret of Victory,* 1926): "... despite the impossibility of physically detecting the soul, its existence is proven by its tangible reflection in acts and thoughts. So with war, beyond its physical aspect of armed hosts there hovers an impalpable something which dominates the material. . . . to understand this 'something' we should seek it in a manner analogous to our search for the soul."

3. Quoted in J. Glenn Gray, *The Warriors: Reflections on Men in Battle* (New York: Harper Colophon, 1959/1970), p. 52.

4. Ibid., p. 44.

5. Careful sociological research into the motivation of the American soldier (in World War II) shows that the factors which helped the combatman most "when the going was tough" (as the quotation was phrased) were *not* hatred for the enemy or thoughts of home or the cause for which he was fighting. The emotions that did appear under battle duress—that is, when Mars was acutely constellated—were prayer and group fidelity. Piety and the love of fellows are what the God brings. (Samuel A. Stouffer et al., *The American Soldier: Combat and its Aftermath,* vol. 2 [Princeton: Princeton University Press, 1949], pp. 165–86)

6. S. L. A. Marshall, *The River and the Gauntlet* (New York: Morrow, 1953), pp. 300–01.

7. "Tomorrow I shall have my new battle jacket. If I'm to fight I like to be well dressed." (Attributed to General Patton, in C. M. Province, *The Unknown Patton* [New York: Hippocrene, 1983], p. 180)

8. Cf. Thomas J. Pressley, "Civil-Military Relations in the United States Civil War," in *War,* ed. L. L. Farrar (Santa Barbara: Clio, 1978), pp. 117–22; Otis A. Pease, "The American Experience with War," in *War,* pp. 197–203.

9. On the slapping incident, see: Brenton G. Wallace, *Patton and his Third Army* (Westport, Ct.: Greenwood, 1946), pp. 207–09; C. M. Province, *The Unknown Patton,* pp. 191–92, 71–86; H. Essame, *Patton: A Study in Command* (New York: Scribner's, 1974), pp. 103–17.

10. Gray, *The Warriors,* condensed.

11. *The Homeric Hymns,* trans. Charles Boer (Dallas: Spring Publications, 1979), pp. 60–61.

12. Gray, *The Warriors,* p. xii.

NORMAN O. BROWN

Born in 1913 in Mexico, Norman O. Brown is one of America's most brilliant postwar philosophers. He delivered a widely-quoted Phi Beta Kappa address at Columbia University in 1961, titled "Apocalypse: The Place of Mystery in the Life of the Mind." Dr. Brown is the author of *Life Against Death: The Psychoanalytic Meaning of History,* "The Prophetic Tradition" in *Studies in Romanticism,* and an examination of apocalyptic thinking called *Closing Time.* In *Love's Body,* he led us on a journey through sex and sensibility in the work of Sigmund Freud. His philosophical explorations range from Greek tragedy to psychoanalysis, and from world-endings in Vico and *Finnegans Wake* to the apocalyptic images of the Koran.

Currently Professor of Humanities at Cowell College, University of California, Santa Cruz, Dr. Brown is writing an appreciation of Islam, its view of history and prophecy.

The Apocalypse of Islam

We can read the *Bhagavad-Gita* in translation, and Confucius; we cannot read the Koran. Carlyle has perfectly articulated the response of every honest Englishman: "I must say, it is as toilsome reading as I ever undertook. A wearisome confused jumble, crude, incondite; endless iterations, long-windedness, entanglement; most crude, incondite;—insupportable stupidity, in short! Nothing but a sense of duty could carry any European through the Koran. . . . With every allowance, one feels it difficult to see how any mortal ever could consider this Koran as a Book written in Heaven, too good for the Earth; as a well-written book, or indeed as a *book* at all."

Louis Massignon called Sura XVIII the apocalypse of Islam.[1] The solemn recitation of Sura XVIII every Friday is all that Islam has in the way of weekly liturgy corresponding to the Christian Eucharist. In Islam the Body is the Book, and the part that represents the whole is Sura XVIII.

Surah XVIII—The Cave
Revealed at Mecca

In the name of Allah, the Beneficent, the Merciful.

1. Praise be to Allah Who hath revealed the Scripture unto His slave, and hath not placed therein any crookedness.

2. (But hath made it) straight, to give warning of stern punishment from Him, and to bring unto the believers who do good works the news that theirs will be a fair reward.

3. Wherein they will abide for ever;

4. And to warn those who say: Allah hath chosen a son,

5. (A thing) whereof they have no knowledge, nor (had) their fathers. Dreadful is the word that cometh out of their mouths. They speak naught but a lie.

6. Yet it may be, if they believe not in this statement, that thou (Muhammad) wilt torment thy soul with grief over their footsteps.

7. Lo! We have placed all that is in the earth as an ornament thereof that we may try them: which of them is best in conduct.

8. And lo! We shall make all that is therein a barren mound.

9. Or deemest thou that the People of the Cave and the Inscription are a wonder among Our portents?

10. When the young men fled for refuge to the Cave and said: Our Lord! Give us mercy from Thy presence, and shape for us right conduct in our plight.

11. Then We sealed up their hearing in the Cave for a number of years.

12. And afterward We raised them up that We might know which of the two parties would best calculate the time that they had tarried.

13. We narrate unto thee their story with truth. Lo! they were young men who believed in their Lord, and We increased them in guidance.

14. And We made firm their hearts when they stood forth and said: Our Lord is the Lord of the heavens and the earth. We cry unto no god beside Him, for then should we utter an enormity.

15. These, our people, have chosen (other) gods beside Him though they bring no clear warrant (vouchsafed) to them. And who doth greater wrong than he who inventeth a lie concerning Allah?

16. And when ye withdraw from them and that which they worship except Allah, then seek refuge in the Cave; your Lord will spread for you of His mercy and will prepare for you a pillow in your plight.

17. And thou mightest have seen the sun when it rose move away from their cave to the right, and when it set go past them on the left, and they were in the cleft thereof. That was (one) of the portents of Allah. He whom Allah guideth, he indeed is led aright, and he whom He sendeth astray, for him thou wilt not find a guiding friend.

18. And thou wouldst have deemed them waking though they were

asleep, and we caused them to turn over to the right and the left, and their dog stretching out his paws on the threshold.

19. If thou hadst observed them closely thou hadst assuredly turned away from them in flight, and hadst been filled with awe of them.

20. And in like manner We awakened them that they might question one another. A speaker from among them said: How long have ye tarried? They said: We have tarried a day or some part of a day, (Others) said: Your Lord best knoweth what ye have tarried. Now send one of you with this your silver coin unto the city, and let him see what food is purest there and bring you a supply thereof. Let him be courteous and let no man know of you.

21. For they, if they should come to know of you, will stone you or turn you back to their religion; then ye will never prosper.

22. And in like manner We disclosed them (to the people of the city) that they might know that the promise of Allah is true, and that, as for the Hour, there is no doubt concerning it. When (the people of the city) disputed of their case among themselves, they said: Build over them a building; their Lord knoweth best concerning them. Those who won their point said: We verily shall build a place of worship over them.

23. (Some) will say: They were three, their dog the fourth, and (some) say: Five, their dog the sixth, guessing at random; and (some) say: Seven, and their dog the eighth. Say (O Muhammad): My Lord is best aware of their number. None knoweth them save a few. So contend not concerning them except with an outward contending, and ask not any of them to pronounce concerning them.

24. And say not of anything: Lo! I shall do that tomorrow.

25. Except if Allah will. And remember thy Lord when thou forgettest, and say: It may be that my Lord guideth me unto a nearer way of truth than this.

26. And (it is said) they tarried in their Cave three hundred years and add nine.

27. Say: Allah is best aware how long they tarried. His is the invisible of the heavens and the earth. How clear of sight is He and keen of hearing! They have no protecting friend beside Him, and He maketh none to share in His government.

28. And recite that which hath been revealed unto thee of the Scripture of thy Lord. There is none who can change His words, and thou wilt find no refuge beside Him.

29. Restrain thyself along with those who cry unto their Lord at morn and evening, seeking His countenance; and let not thine eyes

overlook them, desiring the pomp of the life of the world; and obey not him whose heart We have made heedless of Our remembrance, who followeth his own lust and whose case hath been abandoned.

30. Say: (It is) the truth from the Lord of you (all). Then whosoever will, let him believe, and whosoever will, let him disbelieve. Lo! We have prepared for disbelievers Fire. Its tent encloseth them. If they ask for showers, they will be showered with water like to molten lead which burneth the faces. Calamitous the drink and ill the resting-place!

31. Lo! as for those who believe and do good works—Lo! We suffer not the reward of one whose work is goodly to be lost.

32. As for such, theirs will be Gardens of Eden, wherein rivers flow beneath them; therein they will be given armlets of gold and will wear green robes of finest silk and gold embroidery, reclining upon thrones therein. Blest the reward, and fair the resting-place!

33. Coin for them a similitude: Two men, unto one of whom We had assigned two gardens of grapes, and We had surrounded both with date-palms and had put between them tillage.

34. Each of the gardens gave its fruit and withheld naught thereof. And We caused a river to gush forth therein.

35. And he had fruit. And he said unto his comrade, when he spake with him: I am more than thee in wealth, and stronger in respect of men.

36. And he went into his garden, while he (thus) wronged himself. He said: I think not that all this will ever perish.

37. I think not that the Hour will ever come, and if indeed I am brought back unto my Lord I surely shall find better than this as a resort.

38. And his comrade, while he disputed with him, exclaimed: Disbelievest thou in Him Who created thee of dust, then of a drop (of seed), and then fashioned thee a man?

39. But He is Allah, my Lord, and I ascribe unto my Lord no partner.

40. If only, when thou enteredst thy garden, thou hadst said: That which Allah willeth (will come to pass)! There is no strength save in Allah! Though thou seest me as less than thee in wealth and children.

41. Yet it may be that my Lord will give me better than thy garden, and will send on it a bolt from heaven, and some morning it will be a smooth hillside,

42. Or some morning the water thereof will be lost in the earth so that thou canst not make search for it.

43. And his fruit was beset (with destruction). Then began he to wring his hands for all that he had spent upon it, when (now) it

was all ruined on its trellises, and to say: Would that I had ascribed no partner to my Lord!

44. And he had no troop of men to help him as against Allah, nor could he save himself.

45. In this case is protection only from Allah, the True. He is best for reward, and best for consequence.

46. And coin for them the similitude of the life of the world as water which We send down from the sky, and the vegetation of the earth mingleth with it and then becometh dry twigs that the winds scatter. Allah is Able to do all things.

47. Wealth and children are an ornament of life of the world. But the good deeds which endure are better in thy Lord's sight for reward, and better in respect of hope.

48. And (bethink you of) the Day when We remove the hills and ye see the earth emerging, and We gather them together so as to leave not one of them behind.

49. And they are set before thy Lord in ranks (and it is said unto them): Now verily have ye come unto Us as We created you at the first. But ye thought that We had set no tryst for you.

50. And the Book is placed, and thou seest the guilty fearful of that which is therein, and they say: What kind of a book is this that leaveth not a small thing nor a great thing but hath counted it! And they find all that they did confronting them, and thy Lord wrongeth no one.

51. And (remember) when We said unto the angels: Fall prostrate before Adam, and they fell prostrate, all save Iblis. He was of the Jinn, so he rebelled against his Lord's command. Will ye choose him and his seed for your protecting friends instead of Me, when they are an enemy unto you? Calamitous is the exchange for evil-doers!

52. I made them not to witness the creation of the heavens and the earth, nor their own creation; nor choose I misleaders for (My) helpers.

53. And (be mindful of) the Day when He will say: Call those partners of Mine whom ye pretended. Then they will cry unto them, but they will not hear their prayer, and We shall set a gulf of doom between them.

54. And the guilty behold the Fire and know that they are about to fall therein, and they find no way of escape thence.

55. And verily We have displayed for mankind in this Qur'an all manner of similitudes, but man is more than anything contentious.

56. And naught hindereth mankind from believing when the guidance cometh unto them, and from asking forgiveness of their Lord,

unless (it be that they wish) that the judgement of the men of old should come upon them or (that) they should be confronted with the Doom.

57. We send not the messengers save as bearers of good news and warners. Those who disbelieve contend with falsehood in order to refute the Truth thereby. And they take Our revelations and that wherewith they are threatened as a jest.

58. And who doth greater wrong than he who hath been reminded of the revelations of his Lord, yet turneth away from them and forgetteth what his hands send forward (to the Judgement)? Lo! on their hearts We have placed coverings so that they understand not, and in their ears a deafness. And though thou call them to the guidance, in that case they can never be led aright.

59. Thy Lord is the Forgiver, Full of Mercy. If He took them to task (now) for what they earn, He would hasten on the doom for them; but theirs is an appointed term from which they will find no escape.

60. And (all) those townships! We destroyed them when they did wrong, and We appointed a fixed time for their destruction.

61. And when Moses said unto his servant: I will not give up until I reach the point where the two rivers meet, though I march on for ages.

62. And when they reached the point where the two met, they forgot their fish, and it took its way into the waters, being free.

63. And when they had gone further, he said unto his servant: Bring us our breakfast. Verily we have found fatigue in this our journey.

64. He said: Didst thou see, when we took refuge on the rock, and I forgot the fish—and none but Satan caused me to forget to mention it—it took its way into the waters by a marvel.

65. He said: This is that which we have been seeking. So they retraced their steps again.

66. Then found they one of Our slaves, unto whom We had given mercy from Us, and had taught him knowledge from Our presence.

67. Moses said unto him: May I follow thee, to the end that thou mayst teach me right conduct of that which thou hast been taught?

68. He said: Lo! thou canst not bear with me.

69. How canst thou bear with that whereof thou canst not compass any knowledge?

70. He said: Allah willing, thou shalt find me patient and I shall not in aught gainsay thee.

71. He said: Well, if thou go with me, ask me not concerning aught till I myself mention of it unto thee.

72. So the twain set out till, when they were in the ship, he made a hole therein. (Moses) said: Hast thou made a hole therein to drown the folk thereof? Thou verily hast done a dreadful thing.

73. He said: Did I not tell thee thou couldst not bear with me?

74. (Moses) said: Be not wroth with me that I forgot, and be not hard upon me for my fault.

75. So the twain journeyed on till, when they met a lad, he slew him. (Moses) said: What! Hast thou slain an innocent soul who hath slain no man? Verily thou hast done a horrid thing.

76. He said: Did I not tell thee that thou couldst not bear with me?

77. (Moses) said: If I ask thee after this concerning aught, keep not company with me. Thou hast received an excuse from me.

78. So they twain journeyed on till, when they came unto the folk of a certain township, they asked its folk for food, but they refused to make them guests. And they found therein a wall upon the point of falling into ruin, and he repaired it. (Moses) said: If thou hadst wished, thou couldst have taken payment for it.

79. He said: This is the parting between thee and me! I will announce unto thee the interpretation of that thou couldst not bear with patience.

80. As for the ship, it belonged to poor people working on the river, and I wished to mar it, for there was a king behind them who is taking every ship by force.

81. And as for the lad, his parents were believers and We feared lest he should oppress them by rebellion and disbelief.

82. And We intended that their Lord should change him for them for one better in purity and nearer to mercy.

83. And as for the wall, it belonged to two orphan boys in the city, and there was beneath it a treasure belonging to them, and their father had been righteous, and thy Lord intended that they should come to their full strength and should bring forth their treasure as a mercy from their Lord; and I did it not upon my own command. Such is the interpretation of that wherewith thou couldst not bear.

84. They will ask thee of Dhu'l-Qarneyn. Say: I shall recite unto you a remembrance of him.

85. Lo! We made him strong in the land and gave him unto every thing a road.

86. And he followed a road

87. Till, when he reached the setting-place of the sun, he found it setting in a muddy spring, and found a people thereabout: We said: O Dhu'l-Qarneyn! Either punish or show them kindness.

88. He said: As for him who doeth wrong, we shall punish him, and then he will be brought back unto his Lord, who will punish him with awful punishment!

89. But as for him who believeth and doeth right, good will be his reward, and We shall speak unto him a mild command.

90. Then he followed a road

91. Till, when he reached the rising-place of the sun, he found it rising on a people for whom We had appointed no shelter therefrom.

92. So (it was). And We knew all concerning him.

93. Then he followed a road

94. Till, when he came between the two mountains, he found upon their hither side a folk that scarce could understand a saying.

95. They said: O Dhu'l-Qarneyn! Lo! Gog and Magog are spoiling the land. So may we pay thee tribute on condition that thou set a barrier between us and them?

96. He said: That wherein my Lord hath established me is better (than your tribute). Do but help me with strength (of men), I will set between you and them a bank.

97. Give me pieces of iron—till, when he had levelled up (the gap) between the cliffs, he said: Blow!—till, when he had made it a fire, he said: Bring me molten copper to pour thereon.

98. And (Gog and Magog) were not able to surmount, nor could they pierce (it).

99. He said: This is a mercy from my Lord; but when the promise of my Lord cometh to pass, He will lay it low, for the promise of my Lord is true.

100. And on that day We shall let some of them surge against others, and the Trumpet will be blown. Then We shall gather them together in one gathering.

101. On that day We shall present hell to the disbelievers, plain to view,

102. Those whose eyes were hoodwinked from My reminder, and who could not bear to hear.

103. Do the disbelievers reckon that they can choose My bondmen as protecting friends beside Me? Lo! We have prepared hell as a welcome for the disbelievers.

104. Say: Shall We inform you who will be the greatest losers by their works?

105. Those whose effort goeth astray in the life of the world, and yet they reckon that they do good work.

106. Those are they who disbelieve in the revelations of their Lord and in the meeting with Him. Therefore their works are vain, and on the Day of Resurrection We assign no weight to them.

107. That is their reward: hell, because they disbelieved, and made a jest of Our revelations and Our messengers.

108. Lo! those who believe and do good works, theirs are the Gardens of Paradise for welcome,

109. Wherein they will abide, with no desire to be removed from thence.

110. Say: Though the sea became ink for the Words of my Lord, verily the sea would be used up before the Words of my Lord were exhausted, even though We brought the like thereof to help.

111. Say: I am only a mortal like you. My Lord inspireth in me that your God is only One God. And whoever hopeth for the meeting with his Lord, let him do righteous work, and make none sharer of the worship due unto his Lord.

In the farrago of Sura XVIII, the bewildered Western mind discerns and fastens on to three mysterious episodes—one cannot call them narratives—1. The Sleepers in the Cave (vv. 9–26); 2. Moses' journey (vv. 61–83); 3. Dhu'l-Qarneyn's wall against Gog and Magog (vv. 84–99).

The Sleepers in the Cave:

> *Ashab al-Kahf,* "those of the cave". This is the name given in the Ku'ran, and in later Arabic literature, to the youths who in the Christian Occident are usually called the "Seven Sleepers of Ephesus". According to the legend, in the time of the Christian persecution under the Emperor Decius (249–51), seven Christian youths fled into a cave near Ephesus and there sank into a miraculous sleep for centuries, awoke under the Christian Emperor Theodosius (c. 437 A.D.), were discovered and then went to sleep for ever. Their resting place and grave was considered, at any rate since the beginning of the 6th century A.D., as a place of worship.[2]

Dhu'l-Qarneyn, literally the "two-horned," is Alexander the Great, as in Syriac legend of the sixth century A.D., in which Alexander says to God: "I know that thou hast caused horns to grow upon my head, so that I may crush the kingdoms of the world with them." In late classical antiquity—in between Christ and Muhammad—apocalyptic syncretism, Judaeo-Christian-Hellenistic, expanding on lines laid down in the biblical Books of Daniel and Revelation, absorbed the figure of Alexander into its sequence of world-conquerors. Gog and Magog are biblical figures of eschatological terror. In Ezekiel 38 and 39, Gog and Magog represent peoples of the north who are let loose, with a great army of countless troops, against the peaceful land of Israel, unwalled and undefended. In Revelation (20: 7), "When the thousand years are over, Satan will be let loose from his prison and will come out to seduce the nations in the four quarters of the earth and to muster them for battle, yes, the hosts of Gog and Magog." Koranic commentary, in the spirit of the modern historian W. W. Tarn, sees in Alexander a prophet of the unity of mankind as well as a world-conqueror, and thus a prefiguration of Muhammad himself. Early Christian tradition, and Jewish tradition as early as Josephus, identified Gog and Magog with barbarian peoples to the north, locked away behind iron gates at the Caspian Sea by Alexander the Great, but destined to break loose at the end of time.[3]

The episodes of the Sleepers in the Cave and Dhu'l-Qarneyn's Wall palpably allude to pre-existent legends. The episode of Moses' journey is more complex. The most bafflingly elliptical of the three episodes—and the centerpiece of the Sura—introduces a new Moses, a Moses who like Gilgamesh and Alexander is committed to the quest for the Fountain of Life: "I will not give up until I reach the point where the two rivers meet" (v. 61). The new Moses, having become a seeker, submits to spiritual direction by a mysterious master who bewilders Moses through a series of Zen-like absurd actions, finally justified by his privy knowledge of the secrets of predestination.

Again we have to do with pre-existent materials, but here the action is positive confusion. In the first place, confusion between Moses and Alexander—not the historical but the mythical Alexander of the Alexander Romance, a complex literary production completed about 300 C.E., giving voice to eschatological dreams close to the heart of late classical antiquity. Alexander goes in quest of the Fountain of Life. By the merest chance his cook discovers the fountain: he was preparing a dried fish by cleaning it in a fountain; the fish came to life again and swam away. The cook jumps in and gains immortality. He tells Alexander the story, but they cannot find the fountain again.

The Koran, with its creative confusion of Moses and Alexander, in a characteristically abrupt and monumental gesture breaks with Judaic ethnocentrism and reprojects the prophetic tradition of a new transcultural, universal, world-historical plane. At the same time by making Moses a seeker, on the same plane as the pagan Alexander, the Koran defines a limitation in Moses and in the Halakhic Judaism of which he is the author: he lacks eternal life. In so doing the passage mobilizes, without naming, the powerful contrast, latent in Jewish tradition, between Moses and Elijah—Elijah the most popular figure in the legendary world of post-biblical Judaism; Elijah who did not, like Moses, die in sight of the Promised Land but who never died, being caught up to heaven in a chariot of fire; Elijah the omnipresent Comforter-Spirit present at every Jewish circumcision ceremony and every Jewish Passover; Elijah the herald and helper of the Messiah at the time of the return; Elijah who knows the secrets of heaven and is claimed as the direct source of revelation by Jewish mystics including Kabbalists. The Koran sends Moses to Elijah's school—"it was taught in Elijah's school," Jewish mystics say.[4]

To represent what Moses learnt in Elijah's school, the Koran has recourse to a folktale, type #759 in Aarne-Thompson's *Types of the Folktale:* "God's Justice Vindicated." Thompson's paradigm is the Christian story of the Angel and the Hermit, very popular among Oriental Christians about the middle of the fifth century: "An angel takes a hermit with him and does many seemingly unjust things (repays hospitality by stealing a cup; inhospitality by giving a cup; hospitality by throwing his host's servant from a bridge and by killing the host's son). The angel shows the hermit why each of these was just." Just as the Koran transplants the Christian legend of the Seven Sleepers and the Hellenistic legend of Alexander into a new Koranic context, so it is drawing here on the vast ocean of traditional Talmudic Midrashic Aggadic wisdom. For example, the Jerusalem Talmud interprets Deuteronomy 21: 18 ff., with regard to the "stubborn and rebellious son," in the following manner:

> God has foreseen that this son is destined to waste and squander all
> the property of his parents, to commit various acts of robbery, to
> murder innocent people and to do all kinds of evil. The Torah has

therefore ordained that it is much better that he dies whilst still unblemished and guiltless. Another passage in the Jerusalem Talmud employs the parable of a fig tree whose owner knows the exact period of collecting its figs. In case of delay the sun will render the figs rotten and worm-eaten. Similarly God knows the proper season for the removal of His righteous from this world.

Conventional Western commentators, who are quite sure that there is nothing new in the Koran, assume without hesitation that the folktale is to be taken literally and all that is going on in the passage is the transmission of conventional Aggadic piety. A detailed study of the Jewish and Muslim theodicy legends by Haim Schwarzbaum shows that Sura XVIII, taken literally, offers nothing new to justify the ways of God to men.[5] What is new is its promotion of Aggadic folklore material to the status of revelation, its transgression or confusion of the boundary separating Aggadah and Torah. And the Koran, if one may say so, knows what it is doing. Schwarzbaum, who is not free from Westernizing condescension—he quotes "the excellent Orientalist" R. A. Nicholson's remark that "Mohammed with his excitable temperament does not shine as a raconteur"—and who thinks that "most of the stories in the Koran are narrated in a rather clumsy and incoherent fashion, full of vague, cryptic allusions and dim references and digressions," recognizes the "admirable clarity and cohesion" of the Koranic version of Aarne-Thompson #759.

The Koran, with characteristic monumentality, reduces the folktale to its archetypal essence and makes evident its folktale form. The Koran makes evident the folktale form and thereby alerts the intelligence to the problem of interpretation. Folktales, like dreams, are not to be interpreted literally. And the content of the folktale—the episodes of the ship, the youth and the wall—tells us in the most literal, even crude, way, three times reiterated, that there is a distinction between "what actually happened," events as seen by the eye of historical materialism, and "what is really going on," events *sub specie aeternitatis,* as seen by the inward, the clairvoyant eye, the second sight. The form and the content of the folktale oblige us, as they have obliged all subsequent Islamic culture, to make the distinction between literal meaning and something beyond—in Islamic terminology between *zahir* and *batin,* between outer (exoteric) and inner (esoteric); between external-visible-patent and internal-invisible-latent; between materialist and spiritual *meanings.* [6]

Sura XVIII is the apocalypse of Islam: the heart of its message, not displayed on the surface, is the distinction between surface and substance, between *zahir* and *batin.* The context in which the folktale is embedded contains further paradoxical revelations for those who have eyes to see and are alert to read between the lines as well as in them. The context obliges us to identify prophecy (the prophet Moses) with the literal or external view of events (the ship, the youth, the wall) and to attribute the deeper view into the hidden reality to a mysterious other servant of God—not a prophet, or a prophet of the Elijah type as opposed to the Moses type. The context also obliges us to associate the mysterious other with the water of life—or where the two waters meet, the water of life and the water of death.

Sura XVIII opens up, silently, majestically, in the heart of the Koran, the question, What lies beyond or after the Koran? For Muhammad is, like Moses, a prophet. Muhammad is the seal of prophecy; what comes after prophecy? Prophecy is delivered in the form of a book, a scripture. But everything including the Book has an exterior (*zahir*) and an interior (*batin*). Especially the Book, according to the Prophet himself. Of Ibn Abbas, one of the most respected sources of Hadith (traditions about the Prophet), it is said: "One day while standing on Mt. Arafat he made an allusion to the verse 'Allah it is who hath created seven heavens, and of the earth the like thereof' (LXV, v. 12) and turned to the people saying 'O men! if I were to comment before you this verse as I heard it commented upon by the Prophet himself you would stone me.'" There is, therefore, a basic distinction between *ta'wil,* the symbolic and hermeneutic interpretation of the inner meaning, and *tafsir,* the literal explanation of the external aspect of the Book. [7]

Sura XVIII became, in fact, in the subsequent history of Islam the basis for the elaboration of a distinction between prophecy and another transcendent or esoteric kind of wisdom—a kind of wisdom which in the fulness of time came to be most notoriously represented by, on the one hand, the Sufi master (*pir*) and on the other the Shiite Imam. Whereas the cycle of prophecy is over (Muhammad is the seal of prophecy), the cycle of *wilayat* continues, which Seyyed Hossein Nasr tells us, for want of a better term, may be translated as the "cycle of initiation," and also "sanctity."[8] For want of a better term: the translation has to be in terms of Western Judaeo-Christian religious experience. "Initiation" is closer to Shiite notions. Sufi masters, on the other hand, are often more like Christian saints. The Shiite Imam represents a principle of authoritative guidance in interpretation of the revelation; the Sufi *pir* represents a principle of mystic illumination which supplements the legislative or imperative mood of prophecy.

The text of Sura XVIII leaves us with a riddle: Who is the mysterious other, "one of our slaves, unto whom we had given mercy from Us, and had taught him knowledge from Our presence" (v. 66)? Although he is like Elijah, he is not exactly Elijah; the Koran with a characteristically majestic gesture leaves him unnamed. The Koran leaves us with a riddle, or an assignment, to find him. The ellipses in the Koran are pregnant with the future. Very soon, within the first century, Muslim traditions and commentary on the Koran had given a name to the "Servant of God" who initiates Moses—al-Khadir, or Khidr, the Green (the sacred color of Islam), or Evergreen—taking their cue not from the reminiscence of Elijah but from the bold Koranic association of the servant with the Fountain of Life in the Alexander Romance.

The name, the Evergreen, while naming, preserves his unnamable, unhistorical or supra-historical, archetypal or folkloristic essence. In traditional Muslim piety Khidr, like Elijah, enjoys eternal life and invisible omnipresence. Like Elijah he participates in the small rituals of domestic life and in the great public liturgies. Every Friday he prays in five different places—Mecca, Medina, Jerusalem, Quba (southeast of Medina) and Tur Sina (Sinai). For the annual fast of Ramadan he is in Jerusalem; for the Hajj (pilgrimage) he is always in Mecca. The eternal protector of the community will appear at the Return at the head of the armies of the Mahdi who will fill the earth with justice even as it is now full of injustice.[9] In Islam the umbilical cord which connects "popular superstition" with avant-garde esoteric, theosophic speculation has not been cut, and Khidr is that cord. The Sufis attribute their illuminations to the inspiration of Khidr: Corbin's book on Ibn Arabi (the mastermind of Sufistic theosophy), *Creative Imagination in the Sufism of Ibn Arabi,* is organized around the two questions *Who is Khidr?* and *What does it mean to be a disciple of Khidr?* The rendezvous of Moses and Khidr becomes the prototype of all those later mystic voyages in the company of a spiritual guide, including—when Western civilization becomes strong enough to absorb into its own system some of the strong medicine of Islam—Dante under the guidance of Vergil or Beatrice.

The post-biblical Aggadah shows the efforts of Jewish orthodoxy to reduce Elijah's stature and to counter the excessive veneration accorded to him in apocalyptic Jewish sectarianism and Christian circles. It was denied that Elijah had ever gone up to heaven, biblical evidence to the contrary notwithstanding. Elijah's habit of revealing divine secrets to pious mortals once earned him a severe punishment of sixty lashes of fire. The Koran goes the other way. Without impairing its veneration for Moses as a prophetic figure, it endorses the eschatological longings and mystic revelations associated with the figure of Elijah, without naming him. But the orthodox Sunni *ulama* regress to the posture of Halakhic Judaism. The official theologians of Islam, we are told, are and always have been averse to these excesses of the popular Khidr belief, even as the Talmudic rabbis tried to put down the popularity of Elijah. "There are two things I hate about the orthodox canonists," says the mystic master Shadhili. "They say that Khidr is dead and that Hallaj was an infidel"—Hallaj the martyred prototype of Sufi mysticism, the subject of Massignon's masterpiece.[10]

Who is Khidr? How much does he know? These are questions neo-orthodox Sunni Islam can do without. The great Egyptian modernist, or neo-fundamentalist, Islamic reformer Rashid Rida attacked the Friday liturgy of Sura XVIII as a degenerate innovation (*bida*), a departure from the original Sunna, the hallowed practice of primitive Islam. Rashid Rida also condemned as subjective interpretation all *ta'wil* which claims to find a hidden sense beyond the literal, and he restricts Koranic exegesis to simple literalist commentary, *tafsir*.[11] But the controversy between literalism and mysticism in the interpretation of the Koran is aboriginal in Islam, reaching into the split in the core of the Prophet's followers over the succession to his leadership. The rejected leader Ali is to be identified not simply with the principle of hereditary legitimacy, but also with the assertion of charismatic authority after the Prophet and inspired interpretation after the Koran. Sura XVIII is pregnant with the Sunni–Shiite split and the whole subsequent history of Islam.

The Koran is pregnant with the future. It is only in the light of later developments that we can find the riddle—the question Who is Khidr?—in Sura XVIII. We need more work like Massignon's, whose demonstration of the significance of Khidr in Islamic Tradition remains a unique achievement. Khidr is the key to the Sura as a whole. The occult spirit of Khidr links up with the Seven Sleepers and with Dhu'l-Qarneyn's Wall. Khidr is the Director of the Seven Sleepers, their watch-dog; together they form a community of apotropaic or intercessory saints whose virtue saves the city, like those ten just men for whose sake the Lord would have, at Abraham's intercession, spared Sodom. They repair breaches in the Wall against Gog and Magog that Dhu'l-Qarneyn built. The weekly liturgical recitation of Sura XVIII is to invoke the spirit of Khidr and join the communion of saints in their action of repairing that wall. The fight (*jihad*) against God and Magog is an eschatological reality but not in the future. In the Islamic sense of time we are always in the last days.

The interpenetration works both ways: Khidr is assimilated to the Seven Sleepers; he is an anchorite who has to flee from persecution and lives, exempt from death, having found the Fountain of Life, concealed in a remote island. The melting or merging—"confusion"—of Khidr and the Seven Sleepers generates mystical, i.e., non-literal, interpretations of that sleep. The literalists, Christian or Islamic, cite the story as "proof" of the resurrection, literally understood as life after death. Seen with the inward eye, to be immured alive in a cave is an image of saintly or eremite withdrawal from the world, taking refuge with Allah; and sleep the image of that extinction of self, that condition of being lost in God which characterizes the saint (*wali*) as distinct from the prophet (*nabi*)—in the Night of Unction, the Night of the Heavenly Ascension, the blessed Night, the Night of Enshrouding which is also the Night of Power; the Dark Night of the Soul which is also the Night of *Finnegans Wake*.[12]

The spirit of Khidr is eschatological as well as mystical. The Sleepers awake at the end of time, to figure together with Khidr in the Return of the Mahdi. History becomes a night, or seven nights. And everything is their sleep: the Seven Sleepers can represent the seven prophets who periodize world history—Adam, Idris, Noah, Abraham, Moses, Jesus and Muhammad. The text explicitly provokes millenarian calculations: "which of the two parties would best calculate the time that they had tarried"; "it is said they tarried in their Cave three hundred years and add nine"; "say: Allah is best aware how long they tarried" (vv. 12, 26–27).

It is Shiite exegesis that has made the most elaborate eschatological interpretations of Sura XVIII. The Sleepers hidden in the cave are the Koranic authority for the Shiite notion of the Ghayba, or occultation, of the Hidden Imam. In the Ithni'ashari or Twelver Shiites, the occultation becomes the principle on which they base their periodization of the whole of post-Koranic history. We are living in the occultation, which began with the disappearance, or sleep, of the twelfth Imam in 874 C.E. and will last till his reappearance, or reawakening, with the Mahdi at the end of time. Modern times are divided into the lesser occultation, which lasted from 874–941 C.E.—in which the Imam, though invisible, was still in regular touch with visible representatives of his authority—and the greater occultation, which began in 941 C.E. and is still our present condition, in which communication with the Imam is irregular, rare, unpredictable, miraculous. In this vision of history, modernity means the disappearance of authority (authoritative guidance in the interpretation of scripture).

The Shiite notion of the Hidden Imam is to be understood in analogy with Folktale #D1960.2. in Stith Thompson's index: Barbarossa, King asleep in a mountain, will awake one day to succor his people. Thus interpreted, the legend of the Seven Sleepers contains a perpetual threat of an eschatological outbreak. For example, the Seven Sleepers are Seven Imams of the Ismaili Shiites hidden in the cave, the womb of Fatima, and guarded over by their watch-dog Ali. The great Shiite insurrection (resurrection) on behalf of social justice in the ninth and tenth centuries C.E., which succeeded in establishing the Fatimid anti-caliphate in Egypt, was commenced in the 309th year of the Hegira, as prophesied in Sura XVIII (v. 26).[13]

Massignon calls Sura XVIII the apocalypse of Islam. But Sura XVIII is a resumé, an epitome of the whole Koran. The Koran is not like the Bible, historical, running from Genesis to Apocalypse. The Koran is altogether apocalyptic. The Koran backs off from that linear organization of time, revelation, and history which became the backbone of orthodox Christianity, and remains the backbone of Western culture after the death of God. Islam is wholly apocalyptic or eschatological, and its eschatology is not teleology. The moment of decision, the Hour of Judgment, is not reached at the end of a line nor by a predestined cycle of cosmic recurrence: eschatology can break out at any moment. Koran XVI, v. 77: "To Allah belong the secrets of the heavens and the earth, and the matter of the Hour is as the twinkling of an eye, or it is nearer still."

In fully developed Islamic theology, only the moment is real. There is no necessary connection between cause and effect. Time does not accumulate. The world is made up of atomic space–time points, among which the only continuity is the utterly inscrutable will of God, who creates every atomic point anew at every moment.[14] And the Islamic mosque discards the orientation toward time essential to a Christian Church: "The space," says Titus Burckhardt,

> is as if reabsorbed into the ubiquity of the present moment; it does not beckon the eye in a specific direction; it suggests no tension or antinomy between the here below and the beyond, or between earth and heaven; it possesses all its fullness in every place.[15]

The rejection of linearity involves a rejection of narrative. There is only one decent narrative in the Koran, Sura XII ("Joseph"), acclaimed by condescending Western Orientalists: for once Muhammad overcame his temperamental incoherence and managed to do it right. The strict sect of the Kharidjis, on this point and on others the voice of rigorous Islamic consistency, condemned Sura XII on the ground that narrative has no place in revelation.[16] The Koran breaks decisively with that alliance between the prophetic tradition and materialistic historicism—"what actually happened"—which set in with the materialistically historical triumph of Christianity. Hence the strangely abortive and incoherent character of the pseudo-narratives in Sura XVIII. Something happened, but this strange revelation manages not to reveal what or why. In fact, the impossibility of history as "what actually happened" becomes the theme of an abrupt interruption in the narrative at verses 23–25—the Sleepers. How many were there? The Lord only knows.

"Recalls of former times" are an integral component of Koranic revelation but, as Massignon's Muslim disciple Nwyia says in his indispensable study of the mystic tradition of Koranic exegesis, "recalls of former times" does not mean history:

> Schooled in the Koran, Muslim consciousness is spontaneously anhistorical, that is to say mythic. It takes up events of the past in approximately the same way as the apocryphal gospels adapt the gospel narratives. When Muslim consciousness takes up for its own ends an event borrowed from the Bible or Judeo-Christian hagiography, it in most cases cannot resist effecting a transvaluation by introducing fabulous details or otherwise transforming the meaning. Passing from one hand to another in a chain of Muslim transmission the historical event evaporates and all that is left is a vague memory submerged in a story which has become mythic.

The use of the term *mythic,* with its Hellenic origins and overtones, may be questionable: I would prefer folklore. But the principle Nwyia is articulating we have seen at work in Sura XVIII.[17] At any rate apocryphal: not obsessed with the question "What really happened?", willing to surrender to the fiction that is more real. Gibbon delighted in the irony that the Immaculate Conception of the Virgin, the Dogma of 1854, is first offered as a salvific image in the Koran (III, vv. 35–36). The Koran, with its angels and Jinns, is pregnant also with the *Arabian Nights* and with Rumi's *Masnavi,* the synthesis of Koranic inspiration and *Arabian Nights* imagination.[18]

In Sura XVIII, in the Koran, there is a mysterious regression to a more primitive stratum, archetypal, folkloristic, fabulous, apocryphal. Historical material is fragmented into its archetypal constituents and then subjected to displacement and condensation, as in dreams. It is a rebirth of images, as in the Book of Revelation, or *Finnegans Wake (FW).*[19] In becoming unhistorical it becomes elliptical: "And they forgot their fish; and it took its way into the waters, being free." The fish appears suddenly from nowhere, as in dreams: no causal explanation, no narrative coherence. The fish becomes a symbolic, or the archetypal, fish, the same one you see on California bumper-stickers or in the mediaeval jingle *piscis assus Christus passus.* Moses and Elijah meet; Moses and Alexander merge, or "reamalgamerge" (*FW,* p. 49), not on the plane of materialistic historicism—what actually happened—but in the

world of archetypal images, that world in which Moses and Alexander meet because they are both two-horned. In Sura XIX, verses
25–26, Mary giving birth under a palm tree on the desert is also
Agar the wife of Abraham; and in Sura III Mary is also Miriam the
sister of Moses. In this condensation, Western scholarship sees
only confusion—Who is who when everybody is somebody else,
as in *Finnegans Wake?* Massignon speaks of trans-historical, or
meta-historical, telescoping; systematic anachronism. Islam is
committed by the Koran to project a meta-historical plane on
which the eternal meaning of historical events is disclosed. It is
that plane on which Moses and Elijah are seen conversing with
Jesus in Matthew 17; that plane on which Dante's *Divine Comedy*
unfolds, and Blake's prophetic books, and *Finnegans Wake.*
History *sub specie aeternitatis.*[20]

There is an apocalyptic or eschatological style: every Sura is an
epiphany and a portent, a warning, "plain tokens that haply we
may take heed" (XXIV, v. 1). The apocalyptic style is *totum simul,*
simultaneous totality, the whole in every part. Hodgson on the
Koran: "almost every element which goes to make up its message is
somehow present in any given passage." Simultaneous totality, as
in *Finnegans Wake,* or more generally in what Umberto Eco called
"The Poetics of the Open Work": "We can see it as an infinite contained within finiteness. The work therefore has infinite aspects,
because each of them, and any moment of it, contains the totality
of the work." Eco is trying to characterize a revolution in the
aesthetic sensibility of the West: we are the first generation in the
West able to read the Koran, if we are able to read *Finnegans
Wake.* In fact Carlyle's reaction to the Koran—"a wearisome confused jumble, crude, incondite; endless iterations, long-windedness, entanglement"—is exactly our first reaction to *Finnegans
Wake.* The affinity between this most recalcitrant of sacred texts
and this most avant-garde of literary experiments is a sign of our
times. Joyce was fully aware of the connection, as Atherton shows
in the most exciting chapter of *The Books at the Wake;* I particularly like his discovery in the *Wake* of the titles of 111 of the
114 Suras.[21]

In both the Koran and *Finnegans Wake,* this effect of simultaneous totality involves systematic violation of the classic rules of
unity, propriety and harmony; bewildering changes of subject;
abrupt juxtaposition of incongruities. Sura XVIII is a good exam-

ple. In addition to the mélange of pseudo-narratives, there are two
intrusive parables ("similitudes," vv. 33 and 46) to remind us of the
Day of Judgment; intrusive allusions to the current circumstances
of the Prophet (his grief, v. 6; his lack of children, v. 40); and one
intrusive pointer on pious decorum or etiquette in speech (vv.
24–25). As in *Finnegans Wake* the Koran rudely insists on indecent
conjunctions. The Sura on Light (XXIV), in the words of Hodgson, contains the most ethereal passage of visionary mysticism jux-
taposed with what might seem some of its most sordid, dealing
with matters of etiquette, with sexual decency, and in particular
with an accusation of infidelity levied against a wife of the Prophet. The whole texture is one of interruption (Joyce's "enter-
ruption"); collision (Joyce's "collideorscape"); abrupt collage, or
bricolage, of disconnected ejaculations, *disjecta membra,* miscella-
neous fragments. The widely accepted tradition is that the Koran
was collected, after the death of the Prophet, not only from "the
hearts of men" but also from pieces of parchment or papyrus, flat
stones, palm-leaves, shoulder-blades and ribs of animals, pieces of
leather and wooden boards. In the words of *Finnegans Wake:* "A
bone, a pebble, a ramskin; chip them, chap them, cut them up
allways; leave them to terracook in the muttheringpot" (*FW,*
p. 20).[22]

Hence it does not matter in what order you read the Koran: it is
all there all the time; and it is supposed to be all there all the time
in your mind or at the back of your mind, memorized and
available for appropriate quotation and collage into your conversation, or your writing, or your action. Hence the beautiful in-
consequentiality of the arrangement of the Suras: from the longest
to the shortest. In this respect the Koran is more avant-garde than
Finnegans Wake, in which the overall organization is entangled in
both linear and cyclical patterns which it is trying to transcend.

Every Sura is an epiphany and portent, and therefore not
beautiful but sublime. Again He speaks in thunder and in fire!
What the thunder said. Dumbfounding. Wonderstruck us as a
thunder, yunder. Well, all be dumbed! (*FW,* pp. 47, 262). In the
Koran as in *Finnegans Wake,* there is a destruction of human
language. To quote Seyyed Hossein Nasr:

> Many people, especially non-Muslims, who read the Quran for
> the first time are struck by what appears as a kind of incoherence

from the human point of view. It is neither like a highly mystical text nor a manual of Aristotelian logic, though it contains both mysticism and logic. It is not just poetry although it contains the most powerful poetry. The text of the Quran reveals human language crushed by the power of the Divine Word. It is as if human language were scattered into a thousand fragments like a wave scattered into drops against the rocks at sea. One feels through the shattering effect left upon the language of the Quran, the power of the Divine whence it originated. The Quran displays human language with all the weakness inherent in it becoming suddenly the recipient of the Divine Word and displaying its frailty before a power which is infinitely greater than man can imagine.[23]

In Islamic apologetics the miraculous character of the Koran is self-evident in the immediate effect of its style, its *idjaz,* literally "the rendering incapable, powerless"; the overwhelming experience of manifest transcendence, compelling surrender to a new world vision.[24] The bewilderment is part of the message: "through the windr of a wondr in a wildr is a weltr as a wirbl of a warbl is a world" (*FW,* p. 597).

How do you start a new civilization—in the seventh, or the twentieth century c.e., with all that history weighing like an Alp on the brains of the living? Out of the rubble of the old; there is no other way. "He dumptied the wholeborrow of rubbages on to soil here" (*FW,* p. 17). Massignon speaks of the farrago of folklore (*fatras folkloriste*) in the Koran. First you trash or junk the old—as in *Finnegans Wake,* or the Koran—reducing pre-existent traditions to rubble. Muslim piety, for whom the Koran is the suprahistorical word of God, is troubled by the question of the relation of the Koran to pre-existent traditions. Western historicism, with its well-honed methods of source criticism—*Quellenforschung*—is only too delighted to lose itself in tracing the Koran to its sources, with the usual nihilistic result: the Koran is reduced to a meaningless confusion. Meaning is attributed to the original sources, but in Sura XVIII it has been "mutilated almost beyond recognition" and mechanically combined "in a most artificial and clumsy manner." Schwarzbaum refers to Muhammad as making a brave show with "borrowed trappings."[25] The notion that Muhammad was a charlatan, who stole from the treasury of Western civilization and passed off his plagiarisms on his unsophisticated Bedouin audience as the voice of God, is still very much alive at the back of Western minds. Witness the latest to come from the London School of Oriental Studies and the Warburg Institute: P. Crone and M. Cook, *Hagarism.*

Muslim piety need not be so troubled, nor Western scholarship so complacent and condescending. Sura XVIII with its imperious restructuring of Christian, Hellenistic and Judaic traditions is not troubled. It is a prototypical model of Islamic syncretism. The Koran is not an operation of high cultural continuity, the *translatio* of the legacy of Greece and Rome (or Jerusalem), or the appropriation of the jewels of Egypt as we make our Exodus, as in Augustine's *De Civitate Dei.* To start a new civilization is not to introduce some new refinement in higher culture but to change the imagination of the masses, the folk who shape and are shaped by folklore and folktales. Prophecy is an operation in what Vico called vulgar metaphysics. The Islamic imagination, Massignon has written, should be seen as the product of a desperate regression, back to the primitive, the eternal pagan substrate of all religions—that proteiform cubehouse, the Ka'ba—as well as to a primitive pre-Mosaic monotheism of Abraham. The Dome is built on the Rock. Islam stays with the dream-life of the masses, the eschatological imagination of the lowly and oppressed. The dream-life of the masses, discarded by the elite of the Enlightenment as superstition—the stone which the builders rejected—becomes in the twentieth century the Golden Bough for the return to the archetypal unconscious, *quod semper, quod ubique, quod ab omnibus.* Here Comes Everybody.[26]

Sura XVIII, and the Koran as a whole, like *Finnegans Wake* shows us pre-existent traditions, Jewish, Christian, Hellenistic, pulverized into condensed atoms or etyms of meaning: "the abnihilisation of the etym" (*FW,* p. 353). Out of this dust the world is to be made new. "We are once amore as babes awondering in a wold made fresh where with the hen in the storyaboot we start from scratch" (*FW,* p. 336). In the words of Iqbal:

> the Koran—
> a hundred new worlds lie within its verses,
> whole centuries are involved in its moments. . . .
> A believing servant himself is a sign of God,
> every world to his breast is as a garment;

and when one world grows old upon his bosom,
the Koran gives him another world!

The Koran is not responsible for the way Islam developed into a closed system, and the dryly rational spirit of the Sunni *ulama* turned all the luxuriant cosmic imagery of the Koran into common-sense prose. In the tragic view of history taken by the Shiites, things went wrong from the moment the Prophet died. The problem is, What comes after the prophet? The question is, *Who is Khidr?* And, *What does it mean to be a disciple of Khidr?*—the question at the heart of Sura XVIII. Pursuing that question, Ibn Arabi said that he had plunged into an ocean on whose shore the Prophets remained behind standing.[27]

1. L. Massignon, *Opera minora*, 3 vols. (Paris, 1969), 1: 107–25, "L'homme parfait en Islam et son originalité eschatologique"; 1: 142–61, "Elie et son rôle transhistorique, Khadiriya, en Islam"; 2: 606–12, "Le Temps dans la pensée Islamique"; 3: 104–18, "Les 'Sept Dormants' apocalypse de l'Islam"; 3: 119–80, "Le culte liturgique et populaire des VII Dormants Martyrs d'Ephese (Ahl al-Kahf): trait d'union Orient-Occident entre l'Islam et la Chrétienté." The translation of Sura XVIII cited in this article is that of M. M. Pickthall, in *The Meaning of the Glorious Koran* (George Allen & Unwin, Ltd.). Pickthall's translation spells *Sura* with an "h"; throughout the rest of this article the word will be spelled without the "h."

2. *Encyclopedia of Islam*, s.v. "Ashab al-Kahf." A juicier account of this "insipid legend of ecclesiastical history," which is often retold early in bed and later on in life down through all Christian and also Muslim minstrelsy, in Gibbon, *Decline and Fall*, chap. 33, sub fin.

3. *Encyclopedia of Islam*, s.v. "Dhu'l-Karnain." *Encyclopedia Judaica*, s.v. "Gog and Magog." G. Cary, *The Mediaeval Alexander* (Cambridge, 1956), p. 130.

4. *Encyclopedia Judaica*, s.v. "Elijah."

5. Haim Schwarzbaum, "The Jewish and Moslem Versions of Some Theodicy Legends," *Fabula* 3 (1959–60): 119–69.

6. S. H. Nasr, *Ideals and Realities of Islam* (Boston, 1972), p. 58, n. 1. Goldziher, *Die Richtungen der islamischen Koranauslegung* (Leiden, 1920), p. 182.

7. Nasr, *Ideals and Realities*, pp. 58–59.

8. Ibid., p. 87.

9. Massignon, *Opera minora*, 1: 151–52.

10. *Encyclopedia Judaica*, s.v. "Elijah." *Hastings Encyclopedia of Religion and Ethics*, s.v. "Khidr," p. 695. Massignon, *Opera minora*, 1: 148.

11. Goldziher, *Die Richtungen*, p. 335. *Encyclopedia of Islam*, s.v. "Islah," p. 147.

12. Koran XLIV, v. 3; XCII, v. 1; XCVII, v. 1. Massignon, *Opera minora*, 2: 354; 3: 104–18. H. Ritter, *Das Meer der Seele* (Leiden, 1955), pp. 588–89.

13. Massignon, *Opera minora*, 3: 104–18. *Encyclopedia of Islam*, s.v. "Ghayba," "Ithna 'ashariya."

14. M. G. S. Hodgson, *The Venture of Islam* (Chicago, 1974), 1: 443. Massignon, *Opera minora*, 1: 108; 2: 606.

15. T. Burckhardt, *Art of Islam: Language and Meaning* (World of Islam Festival Trust, 1976), p. 19.

16. W. M. Watt, *Bell's Introduction to the Qur'an* (Edinburgh, 1977), p. 46.

17. P. Nwyia, *Exégèse coranique et langage mystique* (Beyrouth, 1970), p. 74.

18. Cf. Massignon, "Le Folklore chez les mystiques musulmanes," in *Opera minora*, 2: 345–52.

19. J. Joyce, *Finnegans Wake* (New York: The Viking Press, 1958).

20. Massignon, *Opera minora*, 1: 109; cf. 1: 143, 3: 143.

21. M. G. S. Hodgson, "A Comparison of Islam and Christianity as Framework for Religious Life," *Diogenes* 3d (1960): 61. V. Eco, *The Role of the Reader* (Bloomington, 1979), p. 63. J. S. Atherton, *The Books at the Wake* (Carbondale and Edwardsville, 1974), chap. 12.

22. Hodgson, "A Comparison," p. 62. Watt, *Bell's Introduction*, p. 32.

23. Nasr, *Ideals and Realities*, pp. 47–48.

24. *Encyclopedia of Islam*, s.v. "Idjaz."

25. *Hastings Encyclopedia of Religion and Ethics*, s.v. "Khidr," p. 694. Schwarzbaum, "Theodicy Legends," p. 135.

26. Massignon, *Opera minora*, 1: 158–59, 162–63; 3: 128, 143.

27. Iqbal, *Javid-nama*, trans. A. J. Arberry (London, 1966), lines 1132–140. Hodgson, *Venture of Islam*, 1: 392. Goldziher, *Die Richtungen*, p. 217.

JOANNA MACY

Joanna Macy is the creator of "Despair Workshops" designed to address the fears and anxieties of the nuclear age. Based in San Francisco, Ms. Macy has also written *Despair and Personal Power in the Nuclear Age, Despairwork, Dharma and Development* and "Taking Heart: Spiritual Exercises for Social Activists" (*Fellowship Magazine,* August 1982).

Learning to Sustain the Gaze

Over the past three years my colleagues and I have worked with an estimated ten thousand people in groups designed to help them confront their inner responses to the imminence of species death through nuclear war or destruction of our life-support system.

The purpose of this work is to enable us to acknowledge, express, and explore these responses in ways which overcome despair, psychic numbing, and feelings of powerlessness. It allows us to help ourselves and each other to stop hiding from the horrors that imperil our survival, to face them squarely and intimately, to *sustain the gaze*—and find in that act new dimensions of efficacy. This work is based on the recognition that repression of our feelings of impending apocalypse is dysfunctional and dangerous in the extreme. Of all the dangers facing us, the greatest peril lies in our denial of them. This denial breeds impotence and isolation, fosters divisiveness and scapegoating, and blocks from our awareness the very data with which we most need to deal.

These thousands of workshop participants (I have worked with about one third of them in person) represent all classes, occupations, ages, and ideologies. Most of them to date have been white, middleclass Americans sympathetic to the peace movement, but those who do not fit these categories respond to the work in the same manner. We are now developing new forms for this work—to broaden participation to include people who do not attend workshops because they consider them threatening, elitist, or partisan. The most promising of these new forms is the intergenerational Family Chautauqua which we tested in Iowa this year with very encouraging results. The work is also now spreading in Europe.

The theory on which this work is based and the methods it uses are described in my book *Despair and Personal Power in the Nuclear Age*. Let me note here that the philosophical foundations derive chiefly from general systems theory (via Laszlo, von Bertalanffy, and Miller) and Buddhist metaphysics (both Theravada and Mahayana). The methods are adapted eclectically from humanistic psychology, spiritual practices from East and West, and neo-anarchist political process.

The results, judging by the testimony of participants and the behaviors they proceed to adopt, show that, given a safe setting and appropriate methods, people are able, ready, and even relieved to confront their inklings of apocalypse—and that the process releases their energy, intellect, and sense of solidarity with other beings and the planet itself. In other words, with the vast majority of the participants, regardless of age, background and party politics, we have found that:

1. People know what is happening to their world. Each has his or her own expertise about what it is like to wake up every morning on a threatened planet. Regardless of their familiarity with the statistics pertaining to the arms race and environmental destruction, they are aware, at a deep emotional level, of the actual and potential horrors confronting our species.

2. The emotions accompanying this awareness include grief, anger, fear, and guilt. Participants discover the depth and intensity of these feelings as they express them to each other.

3. Given their cultural conditioning, most have tended to view these responses as pathological and to hide them like a secret shame. They find relief and validation when these responses are affirmed as sane, normal, even honorable.

4. After working together, they find it appropriate to identify these feelings as their "pain for the world" and to see this pain as evidence of their interconnectedness with the world. By virtue of their capacity to *suffer with* the world (the literal meaning of *compassion*, "to suffer with"), they realize their coherence or interexistence, like cells in a larger body.

5. Through this understanding, and certain breathing and imaging exercises, people learn how to carry this compassion or pain

for the world. They generally prefer, then, to continue to experience it rather than to be relieved of it at the price of a sense of personal isolation. This choice, enhancing self-esteem and extending the sense of identity, is often accompanied by a kind of joy, at times even hilarity. It fosters a sense of community, courage, and commitment to social action.

It is to be noted therefore that this work involves more than catharsis. Because the repressed material represents concerns extending beyond the separate ego with its individual needs and wants, its release can be the occasion for a basic shift in the person's self-image. It opens the person to the wider dimensions of his or her existence. It constitutes both proof of and doorway into his/her sense of interexistence with other beings, like neurons in a larger neural net, the web of life. It serves to redefine, thereby, the basics of that person's power.

In allowing this to happen, the arc or plot-line of the work follows three stages:

1. *Despairwork.* Here we evoke and consciously confront the realities of our planet-time—including the threat of nuclear war, the poisoning of our life-support system, and the suffering of our fellow beings—and we acknowledge and experience, express and validate our felt responses to these realities.

2. *The Turning.* Here the collective nature of our pain for our world is recognized as evidence of our interexistence, revealing the larger transpersonal context or matrix of our lives. At this turning point, we realize that the web of life, in which our pain is rooted, can serve also as the basis for our power or synergy as interconnected open systems.

3. *Empowerment.* In the last section of the arc, we then explore the nature of this power or synergy. We do this on two levels, personal and social, or we could call them spiritual and pragmatic. In the first we explore ways of opening and deepening our perceptions of the resilient resources of the larger web. In the second, we apply these perceptions to our work for social change as we develop approaches, visions, and plans, so that each participant can emerge from the workshop able to take concrete and immediate steps.

In teaching us how to confront the horrors facing us and sustain the gaze, the work allows us to rediscover the original and literal meaning of *apocalypse:* "to uncover, to disclose, to reveal."

The groupwork itself uncovers fresh insights into the nature of reality, into our interdependence, and into what this means for our resilience and our power to act.

Beyond this, new forms of collective behavior are arising which show what people can do when they boldly face apocalypse. These forms promise to play a significant role in our chances of averting planetary disaster. In closing let me mention two that particularly struck me in the course of my recent workshop tour in Britain. They are arising in the United States also, but developed first in Europe.

One is the "walk." From Copenhagen to Paris, from Cardiff to Greenham Common, from Faslane (Polaris base in Scotland) to London, from Seattle to Moscow—in increasing numbers men, women, and children are taking to the road to express their demand for an end to nuclear weaponry. It is very simple: they just drop business-as-usual and walk. They also talk and sing and hold meetings en route; along the way others join them, and their numbers swell. Intersecting with a variety of these walks in the course of my work, I have a growing sense of historical déjà vu. That is, I see them as analogous to the great tradition of pilgrimage.

Through the interactions, connections, and behaviors they generate, they are becoming, I suspect, functionally equivalent to the pilgrimages of the Middle Ages that played so formative a role in the flowering of Western civilization. They also trigger memories of those pilgrimages I knew in South Asia, be they Vinoba Bhave's walks for land redistribution or the gleeful Buddhist mass junkets to sacred sites in Sri Lanka. In the sharing of high spirits and physical hardship, in a combination of roadgang, picnic, crusade, and traveling circus, people rediscover deep resources in themselves and each other—and spin webs of relationship that do not evaporate once they return home.

Another new form of apocalyptic or "uncovering" behavior that arises when people sustain the gaze is the peace camp. This phenomenon began with a walk. The women walked ten days from Cardiff in Wales to the U.S.A.F. base in Greenham Common to protest the basing of Cruise missiles there. When, upon their arrival September 5, 1981, they demanded a publicly televised debate on the issue, they were denied and peremptorily told "you can stay here all night" by the gate and still not interrupt the NATO plans.

They *did* stay the night and they're still there, a permanent encampment protesting the deployment of first-strike weapons. They are still there despite repeated eviction attempts which leave them living under plastic sheeting through the winter months. Their numbers grow on weekends when ordinary citizens sympathetic to their views come with sleeping bags to join them. On occasions such as planned demonstrations or blockades, these numbers have grown to seventy thousand people.

Over the last year, twenty other such camps have sprung up around Britain, and now they are beginning in the United States (as at the Trident base in Washington, and in Seneca Falls, New York) and in Canada (as near the Cruise missile testing site in Alberta). They offer new ways in which people can be together —telling stories, sharing goods, training in nonviolence. In the character of their commitment, there is a strong spiritual flavor, both ascetic and joyous.

The immediate and primary function of these peace camps seems not so much to disrupt as to educate, to raise the public's awareness of what nuclear bases mean to the future of our species. The sheer fact that these camps are permanent—peopled by fellow citizens ready to sacrifice their conventional comforts—seems to have a public impact far greater than do sporadic protests. Yet I see in them the germ of a more significant long-term enterprise, one which will have a crucial role to play if and when we manage to disarm.

For when the last nuclear weapon, munitions plant, and reactor are dismantled, there will remain radioactive wastes and radioactive cores that must be guarded carefully for the next quarter million years if our species is not to be decimated by cancer epidemics and genetic mutations. What better way to guard these sources of catastrophe than by committed, even monastic encampments or spiritual centers. There a new kind of religious vocation or priesthood can arise, similar to the role that the monasteries played during the Dark Ages in Europe, when communities like Iona and Lindisfarne kept the flame of learning alive. Here, in our awaiting future, these religious encampments will preserve the knowledge of our responsibility to guard against nuclear disaster. Guarding the remains of the uranium and plutonium from negligence or terrorists, they will help our future generations to remember. Coming in retreat to these centers, we will meditate on our powers—our genius and our capacity to commit collective suicide—and we will remember how close we came to disaster. That recollecting is integral to the very meaning of religion (*religare,* "to re-member"). And in such a way, for all the years to come, can our species continue to find in the apocalypse of our time a source of guidance and revelation.

MIKE PERLMAN

Mike Perlman recently received his Ph.D. in depth psychology, mythology and religion from the University Professors Program at Boston University. He has published several articles on archetypal psychology and the nuclear threat and works in the disarmament movement.

When Heaven and Earth Collapse
Myths of the End of the World

In the last millisecond of the earth's existence—the last man will see something very similar to what we have seen.[1]

It occurred to some of those working on the first nuclear bomb
that there was a chance—figured at no more than one in three
million—that the intense heat generated by the nuclear explosion
might ignite the nitrogen in the atmosphere, or the heavy hydrogen
in seawater, thus burning up the planet. This improbable end of
the world did not come to pass, but it remains an open question
whether that first nuclear bomb may have started a process leading
to a holocaust. About fifteen years after this initial vision of a
nuclear end, one of the great psychological thinkers of our century
is said to have had very pessimistic visions of humanity's future
shortly before he died. This man—C. G. Jung—has not been the
only elder of our society to have such thoughts or visions.[2]
Another example—a man from a quite different background—is
Admiral Hyman Rickover, who upon his retirement from the Navy
in 1982 said that "we'll probably destroy ourselves" with nuclear
weapons.[3]

The developments of the nuclear age make it possible that the
end of the world—one of the soul's most archaic and compelling
fantasies—may at any moment become our actual fate. The fantasies just cited, a world-fire and the prophecies of world-
destruction spoken by the elders of a culture, have a psychic
history that predates the realities of the nuclear age. The scientists'
vision of nitrogen and heavy hydrogen ignited by nuclear heat is

perhaps the most elemental form of the nuclear fantasy: the emergence of the fire hidden in earth, air and water—the Heraclitean fire which James Hillman cites in his contrast of the martial and nuclear imaginations. Consider also the New Testament vision given us in 2 Peter 8: 10: "But the day of the Lord will come like a thief, in which the heavens will pass away with a roar and the elements will be destroyed with intense heat, and the earth and its works will be burned up."

Though this passage is the only one in the Bible envisioning a total holocaust, such an event occurs in many end-of-the-world myths, revealing an awful power in the makeup of the world. The theme of a culture's elders or wise men prophesying doom is no less common. In our time, old men of the Hopi and other Native American tribes foretell the end, sometimes including nuclear bombs or world-famine in their fantasies. Aboriginal tribesmen of Australia, as related below, have also warned of the world's coming collapse. This phenomenon is not limited to the modern era: in the sixteenth century, a Spanish missionary in Mesoamerica recorded a belief among Mayan elders that the invading Spaniards would die and that a new world-era would follow in which the "gods would send another new sun" to light the renewed Mayan culture—an allusion to common Mesoamerican myths about successive world-destructions and re-creations. [4]

Our terrifying contemporary realities bear within themselves timeless themes of imagination—patterns whose inherent power manifests in the compulsions of our nuclear dread. Facing these patterns as revealed in end-of-the-world myths enables us to place our contemporary peril in a psychic context. This may help us avoid taking the nuclear danger—and the accompanying prophecies of figures such as Jung and Rickover—only literally. And, as Robert Bosnak points out, we may help to lessen the actual danger of acting out fantasies of world-destruction by acknowledging and experiencing the secret hope and fascination which always accompanies the dread of the end-time.

Yet we should not take too much comfort here. Though we are not the first to be compelled by images of the end-time, we may become the last. In some versions of the most recent stories of the end of the world—predictions of a nuclear winter—humankind succeeds in doing itself in. No New Creation to follow. And no new end-of-the-world myths either.

In the world's earlier mythic traditions, says Mircea Eliade, "the end of the world is never absolute; it is always followed by a new, *regenerated* world."[5] Perhaps this is a hint that there is something essential in end-of-the-world mythologies; there is a renewal and regeneration we find only within the "worlds" disclosed by myths of the world's end. It is not that we necessarily win through to a "higher" level of consciousness or global "new age"; the renewal is inherent in the psyche's unending propensity to imagine an ultimate end.

The end-of-the-world myths that follow are retold not only in a spirit of concern for our threatened world, but also out of the conviction that the world will not be saved apart from the imaginal modes of its ending. We need to save as well the end of the world. This work is a homeopathic way of healing for our predicament, a way of carrying on the task of "Facing Apocalypse." The apocalyptic has a thousand thousand faces, as David Miller says, and the apocalypse is just one of numberless mythic traditions of the end of the world. In what follows I retell several of the essential stories of the apocalyptic tradition, but the reader will also find myths from other, widely divergent world-traditions. This collection is neither a complete nor a representative one, but is meant to reveal some of the variety of end-time worlds. There are many familiar themes, such as the world-fire or flood, a cosmic battle of divine forces, the collapse of the cosmic supports of earth and heaven, and the renewal or re-creation of the world. Yet each myth ends the world in a particularized manner, with imagery specific to the respective cultures and their settings. These particularities are yet relevant to our own culture and predicament, opening us to deeper and more varied ways of imagining—and perhaps saving—our present end-time world(s).

I will not comment further on how and what these myths signify, leaving the reader to explore their many faces. To aid in this I have kept my own comments to the minimum necessary to identify certain themes or explain possibly unfamiliar terms and traditions found in the tales. For the myths speak quite well for themselves.

Native American Myths of the End

Native American myths frequently tell of a time of world-destruction by flood, fire or both. Often this has already taken place—sometimes repeatedly—and it leads to the world we now inhabit. Following are three tales from tribes living in the United States.

The Flathead Indians of western Montana say that before creation the first man, Amotken, was born "to a very powerful woman" who dwells beyond the waters.[6] Amotken lives at the peak of a high mountain, the summit of the earth's covering. He created all the worlds—heaven, earth, the lower world and the worlds that surround these three. Amotken also made the first people, but they soon became wicked, disobeying his teachings. Angry, he sent a flood and drowned them all. But Amotken then made a second tribe, "twice as tall as the first. But they became even more wicked than the first people, and so Amotken destroyed them by fire from heaven."

Amotken then created a third tribe but destroyed these people with a pestilence when they too became wicked. He fashioned a fourth people, who also would have been destroyed had not his mother urged him to spare them. Amotken relented and promised never to destroy his creation again. Those whom he spared were the ancestors of the peoples now living.

The Bella Bella, a Pacific Northwest tribe, say that "in the beginning the people were made by the Chief Above."[7] But as yet there was only moonlight, and the Chief Above had to make the sun. This new sun was too hot, or, as the people thought, the sky was too low. So they appealed to the Chief Above to lift up the sky, and they made a new, better sun. At that time Raven went with his brothers on a trip into the woods far inland. They stopped and went to sleep, and when they woke Raven said: "I had a terrible dream. Run away brothers. I had a terrible dream." His brothers asked him what it was, but he would only repeat, "I had a terrible dream." When they came to a lake, he explained further, saying "Flames," but meaning to say, "The world is burning." At this Raven's brothers jumped into the water, while Raven flew upward. His brothers became water insects then; "the clams were burnt and since that time they have black points; the rocks and mountains cracked and since that time they have deep canyons and precipices."

Some people survived the fire and began to multiply again. But then there came a great flood. Some knew the waters would rise and sought safety on two mountains. One of the mountains was too low, and so the other mountain threw a mass of rock over to it to make it higher and keep it from drowning. People who made it to these mountains were saved.

The Jicarilla Apache say that the earth's center is near Taos Pueblo (in New Mexico).[8] "Some time, at the end of the world, that place will start to burn. The fire will spread to all the world."

This refers to prophecies contained in the Jicarilla origin myth. In that story, the world and its inhabitants were created by the Hactcin, or spirit beings. For a time, the Hactcin lived on earth among men (who were all exactly alike). But one day the Hactcin saw the sky on fire, glowing red as though from a huge forest fire. Then they made ready to ascend and put out the sky-fire, and said to the people that "Before we go we will make you all different." This they did, then left and put out the fire; never again were they seen by men.

"Rocks are alive." Though the Hactcin have left the earth, all things live—rocks, trees, grass, plants, water, fire. They have power and can help us if we treat them well, but they will harm us if we treat them badly. The white man, however, does not know this.

Some day the earth will no longer be able to sustain life, and at that time the people (the Jicarilla) will "ascend to a third place above the present earth and sky, just as they came from the underworld." The sun and moon will also rise to the new place, and the people will follow them. Some of the material from which this earth was made is left over—there is enough for "two more earths and skies"—and is being watched by the Hactcin.

The present earth has already been destroyed once, by a great flood. The next time it will be fire. When this time comes, Killer-of-Enemies (the Jicarilla culture-hero) will come to instruct the people on how to make the trip to the next world. "The earth to which we will go is not yet made. It will have to be made of the material which is being saved."

The indigenous peoples of Mesoamerica have told many similar myths about successive world-ages. Here I will relate two of these, one from the Aztec tradition and one from the Mayan.

The Aztecs, "People of the Sun," held that, at the beginning of the present world-era, the Sun refused to move until a sacrifice was made.[9] Then one of the Gods, Nanahuatzin ("the Pimply One," God of syphilis), cast himself into a huge fire; thus the new world-cycle began. But like the four world-ages that came before, this one will end in universal destruction.

The Aztecs imagined the successive world-ages as "Suns," with the power of the Sun being carried by a different element in each. According to the text *Teotlatolli, Teocuilcatl* (Divine Words, Divine Songs), heaven and earth were "founded" "in the year 1-Rabbit." In this, the first age, the God Quetzalcoatl, the plumed serpent, fashioned men from ashes. This Sun's sign was 4-water; its creation, character and ending were dominated by this element. At the end of this age the waters swept everything away; "The people were changed into fish."

The sign of the second Sun was 4-Tiger—the tiger representing the element earth. In this time, the beings inhabiting the earth were giants. But one day the sun left its course, bringing night at noon. "Tigers ate the people."

The third Sun was 4-Rain-of-Fire. The people who lived in that time were burnt up by a fiery rain, when "the big rocks became red," and the element fire incinerated all things.

The fourth Sun, 4-Wind, ended with a universal hurricane which swept everything away—destruction by air. Those who survived were scattered over the mountains and became monkeys.

The fifth, or present, Sun has movement as its sign and is thus called 4-Movement. For it was the sacrifice of Nanahuatzin which started the Sun moving in its course, and movement will characterize this Sun's end. "The old ones go about saying,/ now there will be earthquakes,/ there will be hunger/ and thus we will perish."

In the sacred book of the Quiche Mayas of the Guatemalan highlands, the *Popol Vuh* or "Book of Counsel,"[10] we find three attempts at the creation of mankind. The third attempt engenders our own ancestors.

The earth and animals were made by the Heart of Heaven who is both Mother and Father. Having made these, Heart of Heaven desired to be addressed and worshiped, but the animals could not talk. Thus, the God formed a creature from mud, but this was useless because it was too soft and melted into the ground. Therefore, it was destroyed.

Next, the Creator made the "doll people," carving the men from wood and making the women from reeds. "But they had no hearts / and they had no minds. / They did not remember their Former / and their Shaper." They were not really human. Thus the Heart of Heaven sought to destroy them as well, sending a thick rain of resin and a black rain which fell day and night to cover the earth. Then the people's animals and cooking utensils rose up against them. "Everything spoke":

> their water jars, their tortilla griddles,
> their plates, their cooking pots,
> their dogs, their grinding stones,
> each and every thing crushed their faces.[11]

Finally the doll people were scattered and destroyed. Even the caves to which they tried to escape shut them out. Now all that remains of them are monkeys.

Next, Heart of Heaven took dough made from maize and fashioned another people, our ancestors. They recognized and honored the Gods, but the Gods were disturbed because these people saw beyond the forests. They were too wise and might become the Gods' equals. Thus, Heart of Heaven reduced their vision to the short and narrow range of sight we possess today.

Impatient Youths of the Sun

There is one type of tale in which the world-fire is extinguished before everything is consumed. Told in various ways by many Pacific Northwest Indian tribes, it has a curiously exact counterpart in classical mythology. Here I will tell the Kwakiutl version of this tale, "Mink and the Sun," and then its Mediterranean counterpart.[12]

One day a woman was inside weaving wool, facing the rear of the house. The Sun, shining through holes in the wall of the house, struck her back. In this way she became pregnant and gave birth to

Born-to-be-the-Sun, or Mink—so named because of his brilliance, and also because people knew the Sun had made his mother pregnant.

But years later Born-to-be-the-Sun was playing with a friend Bluebird, who teased him, saying he had no father. Humiliated, Born-to-be-the-Sun ran to his mother in tears. So she told him that his father was the Sun, and the boy at once wished to visit this father whom he had never met. His mother asked his uncle to make arrows for Born-to-be-the-Sun so the boy could climb to the upper side of the sky. The uncle agreed and made four arrows, giving them to the boy. Born-to-be-the-Sun shot up the first arrow, and it lodged in the sky. He shot up the next arrow, and it stuck in the nock of the first one. When he had done the same with the next two arrows, they formed a chain which reached the ground. He shook this chain and it became a rope; Born-to-be-the-Sun climbed it and reached the upper world.

Upon arriving, he met another boy who asked why he had come to that place. "I came to see my father," said Born-to-be-the-Sun, and the other boy went to the Sun in his nearby house to tell him of this. "Ah, ah, ah! indeed! I obtained him by shining through. Go ask him if he will come in," replied the Sun to the boy. When Born-to-be-the-Sun arrived, his father welcomed and took care of him, saying, "Thank you, child, that you will change feet with me. I have tried not to be tired from walking to and fro every day. Now you shall go, child." The Sun dressed up the boy to take his place but cautioned him: "Don't look right down to those below us, else you will do mischief." Again, Sun said: "Don't show yourself [through] entirely when you are peeping through the clouds."

The younger Sun started on his journey, passing through morning and into the afternoon. Then, becoming warmer, Born-to-be-the-Sun desired to peep through and so swept away his aunts, the clouds. "Already this world began to burn. There was noise of the crackling of mountains, and the sea began to boil. The trees of the mountains caught fire. Therefore, there are no good trees on the mountains and therefore the rocks are cracked."

Furious, the Sun pursued the youth and took away his costume. "Is this what I told you [to do]?" he asked. Then he took Born-to-be-the-Sun by the neck and threw him down to this world, where he landed in water and was discovered by some people in a canoe, who touched his head with their paddle. Then the youth awoke and said, "Indeed, I have been asleep for a long time."

Ovid relates for us the Mediterranean counterpart of this story. One day the Sun, Phoebus (the Sun-God Apollo), struck the nymph Clymene with his rays, making her pregnant with Phaethon, "the brilliant."[13] Phaethon, like the Kwakiutl youth, grew up never meeting his father, though his mother had told him this father was the Sun who brings light to the great universe. Phaethon was given to boasting about his father, and one day a companion, Epaphus—himself a son of Jupiter—scorned him for "believing every word your mother tells you,/ . . . all swelled up about your phony father." And since Phaethon had never met Phoebus, he could not be sure that Epaphus was not right. Maybe his mother had lied to him. In doubt and humiliation, Phaethon went to his mother, and Clymene reassured him, suggesting that he go visit his father and see for himself. Delighted, Phaethon journeyed to the East, "already imagining himself in Heaven. . . ."

Arriving at the great palace of the Sun, Phaethon was dazzled by its brilliance and trembled at "all the strangeness." Phoebus Apollo greeted him and asked him why he had come. Phaethon told him of his doubts and suspicions, and his father reassured him, backing his word with a promise—an oath sworn by the Styx—to grant the youth one wish of his choice. At once, the boy's eyes fastened on the nearby chariot of the sun, glittering jewel-like in the palace light. Too late, Apollo tried to persuade Phaethon to ask another favor, but the youth insisted that he must drive the chariot for one day, harnessing its four winged horses. "What you want, my son," said Phoebus, "is dangerous; you ask for power/Beyond your strength and years: your lot is mortal,/But what you ask beyond the lot of mortals." Phaethon would not listen, leaving his father to caution him to keep a middle course, neither too high nor too low.

After the rosy Goddess of Dawn arrived, Phaethon mounted the chariot and the horses bore it aloft. Quickly they sensed his inexperience and panicked; the chariot careened out of control, first going too high and then too low, setting the earth on fire. "The great cities/Perish, and their great walls; and nations perish/With all their people: everything is ashes." The terrified Phaethon sees the earth on fire, but can do nothing. Finally the Goddess Earth spoke in indignation and fear, asking Jupiter, "Is this what I deserve?" She warned, "If sea and land and sky are lost, we are hurled/Into the ancient chaos. Save us, father;/Preserve this residue; take thought, take counsel/For the sum of things." Jupiter called together the Gods, then took a thunderbolt and struck the careening charioteer from the sky. Phaethon's broken body fell into the arms of a river God. Now his gravestone has this epitaph: "Here Phaethon lies,/Who drove his father's chariot; if he did not/Hold it, at least he fell in splendid daring."

The Hindu "Interval of Destruction"

The spiritual warrior Arjuna, being instructed in the *Bhagavad Gita* by Krishna about the universal essence of things, is captivated by Krishna's description of himself as this vast Oneness. More, Arjuna yearns to see for himself: "to see thy form as God of this all."[14] Krishna, an avatar of the great God Vishnu, grants Arjuna his wish, giving him the divine vision that will enable him to perceive and withstand the power of the God's full grandeur.

Then Vishnu removed his human semblance and Arjuna exclaimed, "How difficult thou art to see! But I see thee: as fire, as the sun, blinding, incomprehensible." Yet the vision also provoked terror:

> When I see thy vast form, reaching the sky, burning with many colours, with wide open mouths, with vast flaming eyes, my heart shakes in terror: my power is gone and gone is my peace, O Vishnu!
>
> Like the fire at the end of Time which burns all in the last day, I see thy vast mouths and thy terrible teeth. Where am I? Where is my shelter? Have mercy on me, God of gods, Refuge Supreme of the world!

For Vishnu is not only the spirit of Universal Love; he is also the God who, at the end of each kalpa or cosmic age, annihilates all beings—even the Gods themselves—in the "interval of destruction" or "night of Brahma" (the creator-God) between the great cycles of creation. Arjuna discovers, with the sacred vision granted him by the God, the awesome end-time of the Hindu cosmos.

In the *Matsya Purana*, Vishnu grants a similar vision to Manu who, during periodic world-deluges, acts as does Noah, saving

specimens or essences of all creatures by taking them on board a
boat until the waters recede.[15]

While Manu was performing a libation one day, a fish came into
his hand. Manu, "full of compassion," cared for the fish, putting it
in a vessel until it outgrew the bowl. "Save me! Save me!" cried the
fish. Manu heard its cries and put it into a larger jar. But the fish
continued to grow rapidly, and Manu had to put it into ever larger
containers. Finally he threw it into the ocean, but soon the fish
"pervaded the whole ocean." The man became frightened and
asked, "Who are you? . . . Whose body could be equal to twenty
thousand leagues?" And he saw that the fish was in fact a form of
Vishnu.

Now Manu, a king and child of the Sun, had been a devoted
ascetic, for which he had been granted the boon of his choice by
Brahma. He had asked to be allowed "to protect the multitude of
all beings, moving and still, when the dissolution takes place."
Vishnu had now come to fulfill this boon, providing Manu with a
boat "fashioned out of the assemblage of all the gods in order to
protect the assemblage of great living souls. . . ." Manu will place
all living creatures on this boat, and in it they will ride out the long
night of Brahma so that they might once more come into being at
the beginning of the next kalpa.

Curious, Manu asked Vishnu, "O lord, for how many years will
the interval of destruction last?" And the great fish replied, telling
him that there would begin that day a hundred-year drought.
"Then seven cruel rays will destroy those few creatures still left,"
said Vishnu, "and seven times seven rays will rain down hot coals."
In the ocean, he continued, there dwelled a fiery mare whose
mouth—at that time bound shut—contained the fire of doomsday.
This will be released after the rain of hot coals, "and a fire will
arise from the third eye in the forehead of Bhava [the God Shiva]
burning and agitating the triple universe [earth, air and sky], great
sage." The sky will heat up with steam, and the universe will be
totally destroyed. "The seven clouds of doomsday—Whirlpool,
Frightening-roar, Bucket, Fierce, Crane, Lightning-banner, and
Blood-red—these clouds born of the sweat of Agni the fire-God
will flood the earth; the oceans will be stirred and will all come
together, and all of the three universes will be a single ocean."

"You alone," Vishnu told Manu, "will remain, when even the
gods have been burnt." With the essence of creatures on the boat of

Vishnu, Manu during the interval of destruction will be with the moon, sun, Brahma, Vishnu and "the four World-protectors, the holy river Narmada, the great sage Markandeya, Bhava, the Vedas and Puranas and subsidiary sciences. . . . " And then Vishnu will proclaim the Vedas to Manu "at the beginning of creation. . . . "

The Doom of the Nordic Gods

Located in a climatic and geographic setting quite different from that of most of India, but sharing a common Indo-European heritage, is the Nordic-Germanic cosmos of myth. Here, too, doomsday is inevitable.

Linking the many realms of Nordic myth is Yggdrasil, the World Tree. This Tree is both forever growing and renewing itself, and being destroyed. A serpent or dragon gnaws at its deepest root, while a hart and goat chew at its branches. But it endures, outlasting men and Gods, most of whom are destroyed at Ragnarok, "the doom of the Gods."[16]

The roots of Yggdrasil are three: extending into Utgard, the realm of Giants; Asgard, the walled city of the Gods; and the realm of Hel, Goddess of the underworld. Encompassed by the roots is Midgard, Middle Earth—a flat disk inhabited by human beings and encircled by the ocean and its monstrous inhabitant, the World Serpent, which bites its own tail until the time when it shall send a flood to sink the earth. But until Ragnarok, the ocean serves to separate the human and Giant realms. Midgard and Asgard, on the other hand, are connected by Bilfrost, a rainbow bridge, which will be broken under the weight of the enemy host advancing on Asgard for the final battle.

Unavoidable as this doom is, several of the Gods' sons will survive; and the beautiful young Baldur, Odin's son and the best of the Gods, will be resurrected. A new earth will arise, and two human survivors of the final flood will begin a new race of human beings.

Just as Baldur will emerge from the underworld after Ragnarok, the end-time is heralded by the approach of his death. This takes place in the following manner. Because Baldur had been disturbed by evil dreams, his mother Frigg had obtained oaths from all the creatures and elements that they would not harm him. But she neglected the little mistletoe—as the trickster Loki discovered. Loki, a sex-changer and shape-shifter, has a sinister side; his activities sometimes help and sometimes hurt the Gods. On this occasion, he persuaded Hod, Baldur's blind brother, to throw a mistletoe dart at the youth, thus killing him. The Gods were terribly grieved at this, and none more than Odin. Not only was his best son dead, but Odin—as foremost God and receiver of prophetic inspiration—knew this as a sign of the approach of Ragnarok.

The Gods tried to bring Baldur back to life, but Loki stymied them. In retaliation, they bound him with rocks and placed a venom-dripping serpent over his face. His wife Sigyn shields him by holding a bowl over his face to catch the drops of venom. But when the bowl is full and must be emptied, the poison drips onto Loki's face and he shudders in pain—an event which we know as an earthquake. Loki is himself a Giant; at Ragnarok, his bonds will be loosed and he will lead the Giants' attack on Asgard.

Loki also has monstrous children, one of whom is the Fenris-wolf, a menacing grey creature who, like his father, is bound by the Gods but will be loosed at Ragnarok, when he will devour Odin.

The end of the world itself will begin with disturbances in the human and natural worlds. There will be three terrible winters—winds from all quarters, snow, frosts, with the sun being of no use and no summers in between. There will be wars throughout the world; "Brothers will kill each other for the sake of grain, and no one will spare father or son in manslaughter or incest."

The sun and her brother, the moon, are ceaselessly pursued by two wolves, and at Ragnarok they will be caught and devoured. The stars will then disappear, and the land will be convulsed with earthquakes, loosing Loki and the grey wolf. The earth will be flooded as the World Serpent writhes "in giant fury trying to come ashore." And then will come Naglfar, the ship of the Giants, made of the uncut nails of dead men. The Fenris-wolf will advance with gaping mouth—his upper jaw against the sky, his lower jaw against the earth. And the World Serpent, coming ashore, will blow poison over all the land.

Midgard, overwhelmed by frost and floods, will be set on fire by the sons of Muspell, Giants from the fiery realm of the south. They will be led by Surt, whose sword "shines more brightly than the sun." The gathering host will then ride over Bilfrost, the rainbow bridge, breaking it. Only then do the Gods, now summoned by a blast of the horn of Heimdall, the divine watchman, awaken to their plight.

After taking counsel, the Gods join battle on the field of Vigrid. "Odin will ride first in a helmet of gold and a beautiful coat of mail and with his spear Gungnir, and he will make for the [Fenris-wolf]." But like the sun and moon, he will be devoured while Thor, God of thunder and sky, battles the World Serpent. Freyr, a God of earth, will battle the fiery Giant Surt and be killed. And yet another monster, the underworld dog Garm, will be loosed and join battle with Tyr, the God who had previously lost a hand binding the Fenris-wolf. These two will kill each other, and so also Thor and the World Serpent. The Fenris-wolf, having swallowed Odin, will be slain by the latter's son Vidar who, standing with one foot on the wolf's lower jaw and placing his hand against the upper, will rip his mouth apart. And Heimdall and Loki, battling, will also destroy each other. As foretold by the "Song of the Sybil," Surt will then have his final victory:

> Earth sinks in the sea, the sun burns black,
> Cast down from Heaven are the hot stars,
> Fumes reek, into flames burst,
> The sky itself is scorched with fire.[17]

But from the depths of this doom, renewal will come. For the World Tree, though shaken, remains standing.

> I see Earth rising a second time
> Out of the foam, fair and green;
> Down from the fells, fish to capture,
> Wings the eagle, waters flow.

Odin's sons Vidar and Vali escape the final fire, as well as Thor's sons, Modi and Magni. Like the greening earth, Baldur rises again, emerging from Hel with his brother Hod. And two humans who survived the fire in a protected wood will be the parents of "so great a stock that the whole world will be peopled. . . ." The golden tablets containing the ancient wisdom will be found once more; and the sun, it turns out, bore a daughter before she was

overtaken by the wolf; this daughter, "no less lovely than herself
. . . will follow the paths of her mother."

Jewish Images of the End

Speaking to the prophet Ezekiel, God reveals what will transpire
when God, chief of the enemy army of Magog, comes with his
legions against Israel. Ezekiel shall speak God's word to the adver-
sary: "It will come about in the last days that I shall bring you
against My land, in order that the nations may know Me when I
shall be sanctified through you before their eyes, O God"
(Ez. 38: 16).[18] God hides himself—until the decisive historical
moment, when his dazzling power is to be revealed. From this moment we derive the classical understanding of the term *apocalypse,*
from the Greek *apokalupsis,* "the removal of a veil of hiddenness."
As in the Nordic tradition, the apocalyptic end involves some form
of ultimate battle.

Ezekiel's visions come to him in an ecstasy; visionary experience
(whether genuine or merely purported) is central in apocalyptic
literature. Indeed, this is part of the *apokalupsis:* the veils of ordinary reality are drawn away so that the visionary may apprehend
the primary realities of spirit.

Such was the case with the Biblical work ascribed to the prophet
Daniel, whose visions (Dan. 7–12) I will relate here. The Book of
Daniel was written in approximately 165 B.C.E., shortly before the
Maccabean revolt ended the oppression of the Israelites by King
Antiochus Epiphanies of Syria. Daniel's visions are concerned with
this historical predicament, but picture its outcome quite differ-
ently, in terms of the great event of the "last days."

The visions of Daniel are four. The first one came to him as a
dream. In it, four great beasts appeared in turn. The fourth beast
was mightiest of all, having ten horns and iron teeth. While Daniel
watched it, another horn appeared, with human-like eyes, "utter-
ing great boasts," and three of the other horns were torn out by
their roots. Daniel, continuing to watch, then saw the Ancient of
Days on His fiery throne; judgment was pronounced on the great
beast with its boastful horn. "I kept looking," he recalled, "until
the beast was slain, and its body was destroyed and given to the

burning fire." The dominion of the other three beasts was then taken from them, and there came with the clouds of heaven "One like a Son of Man," to whom dominion over all the nations was given.

The first three beasts, explained an angel to Daniel, were three kingdoms. The fourth was "a fourth kingdom on earth, which will be different from all the *other* kingdoms, and it will devour the whole earth and tread it down and crush it." The boastful horn, this kingdom's final and greatest tyrant, will be cast down. Then all kingdoms can come under the dominion of "the people of the saints of the Highest One" and "serve and obey Him."

In the second vision that came to Daniel, a great goat overcomes a ram, and the goat's large horn is broken, with four new horns emerging. One of these will grow south and east toward the Holy Land, rising up so high that it will cause some of the stars to fall and magnifying "*itself* to be equal with the Commander of the heavenly host. . . ." It will cause the regular sacrifice at the Temple of Jerusalem to cease, a transgression to last 2,300 days. The kingdoms and events represented by these figures are explained to Daniel by the angel Gabriel, and all of this represents "what will occur at the final period of the indignation . . . the appointed time of the end." But the final tyrant "will be broken without human agency."

Years later, Gabriel reappeared to Daniel and spoke once more of the final "desolations." And again, the angel Michael gives a message to Daniel during the reign of the Persian king Cyrus. Wars will erupt, warns Michael, and a king of the north will gain great power and exalt himself, "speaking monstrous things against the God of gods." "And there will be a time of distress such as never occurred since there was a nation until that time. . . ." Only then will come the final redemption and judgment, with the righteous gaining everlasting life. The time of distress is to last 1,290 days. "But as for you," Michael says to Daniel, "go *your* way to the end; then you will enter into rest and rise *again* for your allotted portion at the end of the age."

These visions have given inspiration to innumerable apocalyptists in both the Jewish and Christian traditions. Here we will remain with the group of Jews to which the writer of Daniel may have belonged, who in the face of the extreme oppression of their time came to believe that the end of the age was imminent.[19] Part of this group left Jerusalem and founded a community in the desert near the northwestern corner of the Dead Sea—the Essenes of Khirbet Qumran, who left for us what we now know as the Dead Sea Scrolls. These documents reveal the apocalyptic and eschatological preoccupations of this severely religious community, and describe the coming final war of vengeance against their enemies, the Sons of Darkness, Belial or Satan—during which these enemies would be vanquished by the Sons of Light.[20] The plans for this war are set out in the Scroll of the War Rule.[21]

Humanity is divided into two camps, reflecting the cosmic duality of God and Satan. Some fall into the lot of the Sons of Light, others into that of the Sons of Darkness. The forces of Light and Darkness struggle with each other both as nation against nation and within each individual, and this struggle will continue until the end-time.

The final war will thus take place both on earth, between (and within) men, and in heaven, between light and dark angels. It will last forty years, but there will be no fighting in every seventh, or Sabbath, year. "This shall be the time of salvation for the people of God,/the hour of dominion for all the men of his lot/and of final destruction for all the lot of Belial." And as the people of God gain dominion over the nations, the light of God shall illuminate, by degrees, the entire world.

But the battle will be difficult. Three times, the Sons of Light will force the army of Satan to retreat; three times, the Sons of the Prince of Darkness will force God's people back. But in the seventh lot, God Himself will intervene, His hand strengthening the heart of the Sons of Light and ultimately annihilating the forces of Belial.

Weapons and infantry must be set out in precise formations. On their "trumpets of pursuit," the Sons of Light shall write: "God overthrows all the/sons of darkness: He will not withdraw His Anger till He has destroyed them." Three battalions shall cast toward the enemy javelins of war, inscribing on their pennants such phrases as "Flashing spear for the Power of God." Before the battle begins, the high priest will exhort the warriors by evoking God's greatness and the glory of His creation: "Thine is the battle!/From [Thee] comes the power;/truly [the battle] is not ours!" After the victory, a hymn of praise and gratitude is to be spoken. Great is the Name of God whose "favours fall upon the rem[nant of Thy people]."

Other writings found at the Qumran site describe the destruction of the world by earthquake and fire: this "shall be final, without anything like it." But there will follow a "time of Renewal," described by the Book of Enoch (a Jewish apocalypse of which many portions were found at Qumran) as a period when the righteous will beget thousands of children and live out their old age in peace.[22]

> And then shall the whole earth be tilled in righteousness, and shall all be planted with trees and be full of blessing. . . . and they shall plant vines on it: and the vine which they plant thereon shall yield wine in abundance, and as for all the seed which is sown thereon each measure [of it] shall bear a thousand, and each measure of olives shall yield ten presses of oil. (En. 10: 18–20)

The Christian Apocalypse

"*A.D.* means All Done," says a man looking back on the Christian era from the vantage point of the post-nuclear world of Russell Hoban's novel *Riddley Walker.*[23] "The time of the Antichrist and of the End of the world will be soon and quite soon and very shortly," says the Spanish Dominican St. Vincent Ferrer, who preached during the years of the Great Schism of the Church (1378–1417).[24]

Christianity has been seen as originating in an apocalyptic movement within Judaism. Jesus himself lived in imminent expectation of the end, and end-time fantasies have pervaded Christianity ever since. Let us recall one of the main sources of this forever-imminent Apocalypse, the Book of Revelation.[25]

Having been exiled by Roman authorities to the island of Patmos, Christ's bond-servant John was visited by Him and shown "the things which must shortly take place. . . ." Christ looks quite different from the Jesus of the Gospels: His hair is snow-white, His eyes glow like a flame of fire, and His feet "like burnished bronze. . . . And in His right hand He held seven stars; and out of His mouth came a sharp two-edged sword; and His face was like the sun shining in its strength." John fell in a shock of fright at His visage. When he recovered, Christ instructed him to give messages to the seven churches of Asia.

Next, John sees the throne of God, from which proceed peals of thunder and flashes of lightning. Surrounding the throne are twenty-four elders and four creatures looking like a lion, calf, man and eagle, respectively. In God's right hand is a seven-sealed book; the Lamb of God, standing "as if slain," breaks the seals one by one. With the breaking of the first four seals there appear the four horses of the Apocalypse, the last one being "an ashen horse; and he who sat on it had the name Death; and Hades was following with him." These horsemen are given authority over a quarter of the earth, "to kill with sword and with famine and with pestilence and by the wild beasts of the earth." With the breaking of the fifth seal, those who had been slain for speaking God's word cry out for vengeance. After the sixth seal is broken, there follows a great earthquake and the sun becomes black as sackcloth. The moon turns blood-red, and the stars fall from the sky on this day of "the wrath of the Lamb."

Four angels stand at the corners of the earth, ready to wreak more devastation. When the Lamb breaks the seventh seal, a silence follows. Standing before God are seven angels who are given seven trumpets; the blast of each will signal yet more destruction. At the first blast, "there came hail and fire, mixed with blood, and they were thrown to the earth, and a third of the earth was burned up, and a third of the trees were burned up, and all the green grass was burned up." In spite of this, and the killing and dying that follow the succeeding trumpet-blasts (with the sixth blast, the four angels at the earth's corners unleash armies on horseback that annihilate a third of humankind), those who survive do not repent of their sins.

At the seventh and final trumpet blast, the voices of heaven proclaim that "the kingdom of the world has become *the kingdom* of our Lord, and of his Christ; and He will reign forever and ever." God's temple in heaven is opened, accompanied by lightning, thunder, an earthquake and hailstorm. There appears too a woman—"clothed with the sun, and the moon under her feet, and on her head a crown of twelve stars"—laboring to give birth to a child. She is attacked by a seven-headed, ten-horned dragon, and a war in heaven ensues, with Michael and his angels fighting the dragon. Helped by the earth, the sun-woman escapes and the child is "caught up to God. . . ."

The dragon—Satan himself—fights with the Christians; a beast comes from over the sea to represent him and is given dominion over all the nations. He is the Antichrist, and all those whose names are not found in "the book of life of the Lamb" will worship him, though he speaks blasphemies against God. But he is the Last Emperor of this world, and his followers shall be condemned to everlasting torment. For it is time for the Son of Man to reap the harvest of the earth, and an angel "gathered *the clusters from the vine of the earth*, and threw them into the great wine press of the wrath of God. And the wine press was trodden outside the city, and blood came out from the wine press, up to the horses' bridles, for a distance of two hundred miles."

The wrath of God is not complete until seven more angels appear and pour seven vials of wrath onto the earth. One of these angels shows John a woman with seven heads and ten horns: the scarlet woman Babylon, the Mother of Harlots and immoral cargoes—all the riches of this world. Babylon and her riches are burnt up in one hour—the cleansing of the Apocalypse. Now Christ appears to John again, astride a white horse and ready to rule the nations "with a rod of iron." With His army, Christ defeats the representative of Satan, together with his false prophet, and the Old Serpent himself is bound by an angel for a thousand years, after which he must be loosed for a time. But at the final judgment, the final end of this world, he will be cast into Hell to burn forever, with all his followers.

"And I saw," wrote John, "a new heaven and a new earth; for the first heaven and the first earth passed away, and there is no longer *any* sea. And I saw the holy city, new Jerusalem, coming down out of heaven from God, made ready as a bride adorned for her husband." This dazzling and bejeweled city is laid out in the shape of a square, with three gates on each side. It needs neither the sun nor the moon to shine upon it, for there is "no night there." The river of life flows from its center, and on either side of the river stands a tree of life yielding each month twelve kinds of fruit whose leaves are "for the healing of the nations."

"Do not seal up the words of the prophecy of this book," an angel tells John, "for the time is near." "Yes," says Jesus, "I am coming quickly." And John: "Amen. Come, Lord Jesus."

At the end, there is something to look forward to. So say the multitude of apocalypses written after, and inspired by, Revelation and earlier works such as Daniel and Enoch. What follows is the description of the end in the apocryphal Apocalypse of Thomas, probably written before the fifth century.[26]

It will take eight days for the world to end, and the last day will be an occasion for much rejoicing. The signs of the end of the world will appear (says Christ to Thomas) "before my elect come forth from the world." The time of these things, though hidden from men and angels, is coming soon. There will be famine, pestilence and war on earth. When the end begins—on the third hour of the first day—"there will be a mighty and strong voice in the firmament of the heaven," followed by a cloud of blood in the north which will cover the sky, bringing thunder, lightning and a rain of blood that will descend over all the earth.

On the second day, the voice will sound again "and the earth will be moved from its place." The gates of heaven in the east will open, and from these the smoke of a great fire will flow to cover the sky, bringing "fears and great terrors." On the third day, the voice will sound and the earth will roar in its depths; acrid smoke will fill the air. The first hour of the fourth day will bring the melting and rumbling of the abyss, and a terrible earthquake will fell heathen idols and the earth's cities. On the fifth day the sun will burst, leaving the world in darkness; the moon and stars "will cease their work." On the sixth day, in its fourth hour, the voice will sound again and the firmament be rent, so that men will be able to see the angels looking down upon the earth. Terrified, they will flee; "such things will happen as never happened since this world was created." Christ Himself will become visible to men as he descends illumined by His Father. When he arrives, the fire with which Paradise is ringed will be loosed to devour the world.

At that time Christ's elect will be resurrected and transfigured, delivered from this world, while—beginning at the eighth hour of the seventh day—there will be a war between angels. When this is finished, on the eighth day, a pleasant voice will sound in heaven, and God's angels, going forth "to deliver the elect who believed in me . . . will rejoice that the destruction of the world has come."

In these stories, Christ's appearance signals the end of the world. There is one story, however, in which this is forestalled. Christ, one day, was making ready to destroy the world with three lances.

But out of sympathy, the Blessed Virgin, along with Saints Francis and Dominic, pleaded with Christ on the world's behalf, thus saving it for the present.[27]

But next time, warns St. Vincent, it will be the utter end: "there will . . . come a fire from East to West by the power of God and not by any natural motion. The whole earth and anything that is in it will burn, so that it will be like ashes in a furnace."[28]

Native Australian World-Endings

Native Australians have long been aware that their activities are what renew the world and prevent its catastrophic end. This means careful ritual attention to, and re-creation of, the sacred events that took place as the present world was being formed and shaped—in the primordial "Dreaming" or "Dreamtime." The laws and traditions by which the Dreamtime is remembered must forever be kept or the world will collapse.

The Wadaman of Northern Australia tell what will happen if the Dreamtime law should be forgotten.[29] A giant, Nada, now holds up the earth. He uses it as a shield, resting it atop his head. In the sky above him, dwelling in a cave by the "road 'on top'" (the Milky Way), is Utdjungon, "the old sky lord." Utdjungon is hostile to Nada and to humankind, watching for the time when he can lash out at them with a fiery meteor, "a giant star,/Striking the earth with a mighty roar. . . ." Utdjungon is held back only because people follow the laws established in the Dreamtime and are supported by Nada, who "holds us up;/'Tis he who holds our destiny,/The Dreamtime law—our destiny—/If we forget, we cease to be."

If ever Nada and Utdjungon should fight, the moon will grow dim and the sun go out. The earth will quake, hills topple, and the world will end. The heroes of the Dreamtime will rise again amidst the clashing, but all people alive will die. And even though Nada will win, it is to no avail, for he will throw away his shield, the earth, which will be turned upside down. The ghosts usually underneath will walk about upon the earth's surface.

So far, the native peoples—especially the Wadaman—have kept the Dreamtime laws and thus held off this fatal fight. But now

(with the white man's arrival) the tribe is dying out; "our springs
have died." How much longer, then, before Utdjungon strikes?

> 'Tis only we who know the law
> Who hold him there in the old sky track.
> Without us none can hold him back.
> Then as he springs, and all goes black,
> This earth will shudder, the trees come down;
> And over the noise you will hear our cry:
> We'll cry for you as you pass away;[30]
> We'll *laugh* at you as you pass away.

The Unambal, a northwest Australian tribe, consider it essential
that its members each year renew, by repainting, certain images
found on rocks and in caves.[31] Some of these are images of plants
and animals which, during the Dreamtime, were projected from
heaven by Wallanganda, the spirit of the Milky Way. There are
also figures, like humans but lacking mouths, called "Wondjina."
The Wondjina, during the Dreamtime, walked upon the earth,
making rain and hills and plains. At that time the rocks were wet,
soft and impressionable. At the end of the Dreamtime the Wondjina lay down on them, leaving their images. Then they entered the
earth, where they now live. They are the spirit-ancestors of human
beings; part of each person's soul is descended from a particular
Wondjina who entered the earth at a specific place. During the
yearly repainting ritual, the person both renews his connection,
remembers his special identity with his spirit-ancestor, and ensures
that new sources of water will be found during the coming rainy
season.

Life and the world have remained as they are because the Wondjina are remembered in this manner. But if their images are
neglected and the Dreamtime teachings forgotten, the world must
come to an end. At that time, the paintings will pale and the rocks
erode and collapse. The Wondjina and Ungud—a great rainbow-
serpent living under the earth—will depart from the world. No
more water will be found; as the sources vanish, all the earth will
become a desert, and slow but certain death will come to
everything. This doom will spread from clan to clan, and when all
life has gone, the stone pillars supporting the heavens will begin to

wobble and sway. Then the sky will collapse. Wallanganda, who had been guarding the traditions, will perish as well, and the world will return to the darkness that was before the Dreamtime.

This is happening now, say the Unambal elders. The people are losing touch with the ancient laws and ancestral images. The world is ending now.

1.   Scientist George Kistiakowsky, recalling the first nuclear explosion. Quoted in Robert Jay Lifton, *The Broken Connection* (New York: Simon & Schuster, 1979), p. 372.

2.   Jung's visions were discussed by Marie-Louise von Franz in the recent film on Jung's life, *A Matter of Heart.*

3.   Quoted in Robert Jay Lifton and Richard Falk, *Indefensible Weapons: The Political and Psychological Case Against Nuclearism* (New York: Basic Books, Inc., 1982), p. 96.

4.   Cited in J. Eric S. Thompson, *Maya History and Religion* (Norman: University of Oklahoma Press, 1970), p. 335.

5.   Mircea Eliade, *Myths, Dreams and Mysteries,* trans. Philip Mairet (New York: Harper & Row, 1975), p. 243.

6.   From Ella P. Clark, *Indian Legends from the Northern Rockies* (Norman: University of Oklahoma Press, 1966), pp. 66–67.

7.   Told by an informant in Franz Boas, *Bella Bella Tales* (New York: American Folklore Society, 1932), pp. 1–2.

8.   Told by an informant in Morris Edward Opler, *Myths and Tales of the Jicarilla Apache Indians* (New York: American Folklore Society, 1969 [rpt.]), pp. 109–10 and 336.

9.   On this point see Joseph Campbell, *The Mythic Image* (Princeton: Princeton University Press, 1974), p. 158. The Aztec text cited below is found in Miguel Leon-Portilla, ed., *Native American Spirituality* (New York: Paulist Press, 1980), pp. 137–44.

10.   Leon-Portilla, *Native Mesoamerican Spirituality,* pp. 101–34.

11.   *Popol Vuh: A Mayan Book of Myth and History,* trans. Dennis Tedlock (New York: Simon & Schuster, 1985).

12.   From Franz Boas, *Kwakiutl Tales* (New York: Columbia University Press, 1910), pp. 123–27.

13.   Ovid, *Metamorphoses,* trans. Rolfe Humphries (Bloomington: Indiana University Press, 1955), pp. 24–26. For a commentary on the psychology of the nuclear threat in relation to this myth, see Mike Perlman, "Phaethon and the Thermonuclear Chariot," *Spring 1983:* 87–108.

14.   *The Bhagavad Gita,* trans. Juan Mascaro (Baltimore: Penguin Books, 1975), 11: 3–25.

15.   In *Hindu Myths,* trans. Wendy Doniger O'Flaherty (Baltimore: Penguin Books, 1975), pp. 181–84.

16. The following account is derived from *The Prose Edda of Snorri Sturluson,* selected and trans. Jean I. Young (Berkeley: University of California Press, 1966); and H. R. Ellis Davidson, *Scandinavian Mythology* (New York: The Hamlyn Publishing Group, Ltd., 1969).

17. Printed in *The Elder Edda: A Selection,* trans. Paul B. Taylor and W. H. Auden (New York: Random House, 1969), pp. 144–53.

18. This and all subsequent references to the Bible are taken from the American Standard Version.

19. The Essenes, suggests Kurt Schubert in *The Dead Sea Community,* trans. John Doberstein (New York: Harper & Bros., 1959), p. 30.

20. This scheme shows the influence of Zoroastrian dualism, which is especially strong in both gnostic and apocalyptic writings.

21. Printed in A. Dupont-Sommer, *The Essene Writings from Qumran,* trans. G. Vermes (Gloucester, Mass.: Peter Smith, 1973), from which (pp. 170 ff.) the following account is taken.

22. Cf. *The Book of Enoch,* trans. R. H. Charles (New York: The Mac-Millan Co., 1935), from which the following passage is taken.

23. Russell Hoban, *Riddley Walker* (New York: Summit Books, 1982), p. 125.

24. This and subsequent quotes from St. Vincent are printed in Bernard McGinn, *Visions of the End* (New York: Columbia University Press, 1979), pp. 256–58.

25. The following account is also based on the American Standard Version of the Bible.

26. The Apocalypse of Thomas is printed in Edgar Hennecke, *New Testament Apocrypha,* trans. R. M. Wilson, vol. 2 (Philadelphia: The Westminster Press, 1965), pp. 799–803.

27. Bernard McGinn, *Visions,* p. 342, n. 24.

28. Cf. Matt. 24: 27.

29. From Bill Harney and A. P. Elkin, *Songs of the Songmen* (Adelaide: Ribby Ltd., 1968), pp. 29–31.

30. This is directed at the white man.

31. From Helmut Petri, "Das Weltende im Glauben australischer Eingeborenen," *Paideuma* 4 (1950): 350; my thanks go to Robert Bosnak for his translation of the relevant passage.

Recent and New Titles from Spring

ANIMA AS FATE   Cornelia Brunner, preface by C. G. Jung

First translation into English of a classic Jungian work by a Swiss analyst. Part I explores the notion of the anima in the work of Rider Haggard, particularly in his novel *She*, but also provides background and a psychological evaluation of the author's life. Part II traces the development of the anima in a series of dreams that a middleaged physician experienced. Jungian Classics Series 9. (xv, 276 pp., ISBN 0-88214-508-8)

PAGAN MEDITATIONS   Ginette Paris

An appreciation of three Greek Goddesses as values of importance to our twentieth-century collective life: Aphrodite as civilized sexuality and beauty; Artemis as solitude, ecological significance, and a perspective on abortion; and Hestia as warm hearth, security, and stability. This contribution to *imaginative* feminism addresses both the meditative interior of each person and the community of culture. (204 pp., ISBN 0-88214-330-1)

HERMES: *Guide of Souls*   Karl Kerényi

The famous mythographer, classicist, and friend of Jung here presents a beautiful, authoritative study of the great God whom the Greeks revered as Guide of Souls. Chapters on Hermes and Night, Hermes and Eros, Hermes and the Goddesses illuminate the complex role of Hermes in classical mythology, while also providing an archetypal background for the guiding of souls in psychotherapy. (104 pp., ISBN 0-88214-207-0)

ANIMA: *An Anatomy of a Personified Notion*   James Hillman

Anima and Eros, Anima and Feeling, Anima and Feminine, Mediatrix of the Unknown—ten succinct chapters, accompanied by relevant quotations from Jung (on left-hand pages facing Hillman's essay), which clarify the moods, persons, and definitions of the most subtle and elusive aspect of psychology and of life. (188 pp., ISBN 0-88214-316-6)

"In spite of the stimulating complexity of this analysis, this book captures and retains the fascinating and living quality of the anima."—*Choice*

A CELTIC QUEST
Sexuality and Soul in Individuation   John Layard

This classic Welsh tale of heroic youth in search of soul finds a master equal to its riddles in John Layard, Oxford anthropologist and Jungian analyst. The quest proceeds as a boar hunt, encountering giants and dwarfs, bitch-dogs, helpful ants, the Witch Hag, until the soul is won. Brilliant appendices, together with scholarly apparatus and a full index, have established this volume as the standard interpretative psychological text of Celtic legend. (264 pp., ISBN 0-88214-110-4)

COMMENTARY ON PLATO'S SYMPOSIUM ON LOVE
Marsilio Ficino, trans. Sears Jayne

Marsilio Ficino, the head of the Platonic Academy in Renaissance Florence and the first ever to translate the complete works of Plato, also wrote this Latin essay on love. Popular in European court-circles for almost two hundred years, this book influenced painters such as Botticelli and Michelangelo, and writers such as Spenser and Castiglione. Jayne's English translation, based on Marcel's edition, includes an introduction. (213 pp., ISBN 0-88214-601-7)

"Jayne's translation is eminently readable, copiously annotated, and contains a bibliography of particular value."—*Choice*

Spring Publications • P.O. Box 222069 • Dallas, TX 75222